A Place in the Heart:
An Environmental Christian Romance

by B. G. Jacques

Copyright © 2005
ISBN 978-0-9834956-3-5
Library of Congress PLN: 2011930891

All rights reserved

No part of this book may be used or reproduced, stored in or introduced into a retrieval system, or transmitted in any form, or by any means (electronic or mechanical, photocopying, recording, or otherwise), without the prior written permission of the author, except in the case of brief quotations embedded in critical articles or reviews. The scanning, uploading and distribution of this book via the Internet or any other means without the permission of the author is illegal and punishable by law.

For permission to quote from this book, address your inquiry to:
SpiritBooks LLC
wilson@spiritbooks.me

For more information: www.spiritbooks.me

Printed in the United States of America by LightningSource, Inc.

1. Christian Stewardship of the earth 2. Nature and Christian Stewardship 3. Malta 4. Southampton, Long Island 5. Pollution 6. Environmental Problems 7. Christian romance

Cover design by Jeffery Shirley
First Edition 2011

For Sally Tibma

Whose love of nature and animals
inspired this book

Table of Contents

Chapter One..1

Chapter Two.......................................29

Chapter Three....................................51

Chapter Four 73

Chapter Five......................................89

Chapter Six......................................105

Chapter Seven..................................121

Chapter Eight.......... 149

Chapter Nine...................................175

Chapter One

It was not the worst day of Rhonna Moran's life, but it was right up there. The worst had been when her dad had his heart attack. He survived, but couldn't farm anymore. Rhonna had known even before the heart attack that the farm's days were numbered. Now she knew exactly what the numbers were. That was why she was standing at the wrong end of a long line at Kennedy International airport, praying for a miracle. From what she was hearing, the plane had been overbooked. So much for her hopes to snag a ticket to Malta and a career as an environmental journalist. Nobody but her father believed she could crash the field. Not even she really believed it, but she was determined to act as if she did.

The big local paper on Long Island had offered her, a mere city desk reporter, the chance to cover the story of Malta's world environmental conference. Stan, their regular European correspondent, had phoned from Rome that he was flattened with food poisoning. Rhonna had once broken Stan's heart by turning down his proposal, and he had taken the European assignment to make a clean break. She felt vaguely guilty, enough to send him a get well card, though it was hard to work up any pity for someone who had a job to die for, especially now that keeping the family farm looked hopeless. The day after Stan called from Rome, Bill Kingsley, the gangling, easygoing editor of Newstar, had called her into his office and told her what he had in mind. Rhonna sat in his office, perching on the edge of her chair. *Please, God,* she prayed, *please let me get that job. You know, Lord, what's at stake. Like everything.*

Bill had tipped his worn leather chair back against the wall, picked bits of lunch out of his crooked teeth, and around the working toothpick, had explained the assignment. A week of world reports on water pollution, dead forests, and acid rain. Could be a stepping stone to something better, Bill added, laughing his huge, gasping laugh, pulling out the toothpick just in time to save himself from a medical emergency.

Her editor never demanded anything, just put it out there. He gave his reporters a lot of room and also, Rhonna had observed, let his wife and kids walk all over him. His eyes were always widening in sudden surprise, and he laughed a lot, usually in embarrassment at his own lack of steam. If he hadn't been superb at jumping on stories that were about to be hot, he would probably be stuck at the city desk too. Instead, he was in a position to offer nobodies like her an occasional plum, like this trip. So, how did Malta grab her, he wanted to know, nibbling another toothpick and eying her from under his thin, silvery eyebrows.

It grabbed her more than Bill could possibly guess, even though for the past year he'd been complimenting her investigative reports on Suffolk County's endangered water table. She'd made a lot of enemies on the water board and among the town's attorneys, but had, in her small way, contributed to keeping the Southampton water supply from salting up through real estate over-development.

Rhonna considered her work a Christian witness and said so often enough that people rolled their eyes and nudged each other when she tried to explain how her faith in God went hand in hand with her love of God's creation. Some of them, though no one in her church, called her "the Witness," behind her back. But in her little community church, many people prayed with her whenever she asked for help in the fight to stop the South Shore of Long Island from growing any more polluted than it already was. Bill went to the same church with his kids and they all prayed together for the land that seemed to be slipping away from them into the hands of rich, uncaring city people.

Bill was aware of how well she could write, but even he could not know what the land meant to her, how she felt when she saw a dead baby seal tangled in plastic fish line or tall pine trees cut down to make way for a new gas station. Sick, is how she felt. And now, a chance to make a difference as well as a buck, maybe enough bucks to pay the back taxes. Oh, it grabbed her, all right.

Thank you, God for giving me this gift. She could barely stop herself from dancing out of the office.

So because poor old Stan in Rome had wiped out on poisoned pasta, Rhonna was standing in the ticket line at the airport, hoping and praying that a last-minute ticket would be left for her, preferably in economy class. She had already put three hundred dollars into a periwinkle blue linen suit that matched her eyes plus a chiffon cocktail dress for evenings that whirled in a rainbow of colors around her shapely legs. It was a perfect dress for a party, though she might be too busy for one. She had had a hard battle with her practical side, making the decision to spend so much money on her image. Her family had always believed in living simply and giving any extra money to their church for people worse off than they were. Clothes were not high on their list of priorities. Up till now, Rhonna had never even considered that she had an image, let alone that she needed to glitz it up. Her only jewelry was a simple gold cross on a chain around her long, slender neck, and sometimes two tiny gold cross earrings that her mother had given her before dying of cancer two years before.

"You have to look the part of a successful world class journalist," said her best friend Megan, a junior society editor, who had helped her pick out the clothes. Insisted rather, for Rhonna's own taste leaned toward white jeans and a navy blue tank top, which was what she was wearing now, wanting to be as comfortable on the plane as an economy ticket would allow.

"If you've got it, flaunt it," Megan said during their argument at the store. She snatched up a short black jersey halter dress and held it against Rhonna's trim body. "And you've got it, sweetie. This'll look great with that black and red Moroccan shawl I gave you for Christmas."

Rhonna looked doubtful. "I'm over my clothes budget already. Any more and I can't afford to leave my hotel room, not even to eat. Some headline I'd make. Flashy environmental journalist starves to death at world pollution conference. A sort of statement, I guess, but not the one I want to make."

"Then I'll buy it for you. Call it an advance birthday present. You've had a rough year, Rhonna. Your Dad's heart attack and the taxes and what all. You owe it to yourself." Megan's round, freckled face was earnest, and she gave Rhonna a little shake. "I want you to knock 'em dead in Malta. Do it for me. Look, you saved my life when those diet pills got to me. I just want to return the favor, okay?"

Rhonna remembered the day she hauled a near-comatose Megan into the emergency room and read her the entire Book of Matthew, even though she wasn't sure Megan could hear the words. She must have, Rhonna figured, since after her recovery, she started going to Rhonna's little church, joined the choir, and was baptized. Her values had changed for the better, but she still loved expensive, showy clothes. Rhonna was trying to help her friend give up this last bit of worldliness, but so far had not succeeded. So, the black jersey and the shawl wound up in her bag, along with photocopied reference articles and her friend's book on Maltese temples to the pagan mother goddess, who looked a little like Megan before her crash diet.

"Look good," Megan insisted, "and you'll be able to take on the world."

Today is definitely not the day I'm going to take on the world and win, Rhonna thought, *however good I look.* Now she regretted that her sense of thrift had lost the clothes debate and that Megan had won it. Much good clothes would do her if she couldn't buy a first class ticket, should there be no more economy seats.

Megan was the only one on the paper besides the editor who knew why Rhonna wanted this assignment so much. If she got the Malta story, she would be able to pay two years worth of back taxes on the farm. She hadn't told her father until just before she left, so as not to disappoint him in case the whole project fell apart. Maybe she didn't have the skill to write anything but stories about the local toxic waste dump or about Southampton's drinking water turning salty as the inexorable ocean pushed its way into the space left by a sinking water table. But Rhonna knew she had to try. Let them call her "the Witness" and laugh at her behind her back. *God is with me, so who can be against me,* she reminded herself, and kept on doing the job she felt God Himself had called her to do.

Ever since she was a little girl trying to save oil-spattered birds on the blackened shore, she had wanted to protect the beauty she had grown up loving and that others seemed to take for granted. Rhonna had taken some courses in Environmental science, but since she had no head for math, a degree in the subject had eluded her. So she settled for a major in communications, a minor in religion, and went on writing about every endangered bird, animal, or plant she could find. Bill Kingsley used to laugh and say if there were an endangered mold molecule, she wouldn't rest until she'd whipped up a public furor against the slaughter of innocent yeasts. Megan had wanted her to buy a short leather suit which would show off her legs, but Rhonna said she would not wear a dead animal and that was that.

At the ticket counter stood a battling fur-coated couple with ten pieces of luggage each large enough to carry a cross-country ski exerciser. It was going to be a long wait. Rhonna sighed and tried futilely to push back the curling tendrils of champagne-colored blonde hair that kept blowing into her face whenever the revolving doors behind her swung, stirring the air. She had had no time to do anything with her hair, which was loosely piled into a thick chignon. The door whirled again now, and she realized some more hair was falling out of the chignon. At this rate, if she ever got to Malta, she would be taken for a refugee from Bangladesh.

Rhonna looked at the tall man who had just created the blast of air by pushing the door hard enough to spin it around twice. He was staring directly at her as if he knew her, his heavy auburn brows meeting over a hawk nose as if he was in the middle of solving a big problem. He was staring not as if he knew her, but as if sizing her up as to what use he could make of her. *Like I'm an unexpected bargain at an expensive store*, Rhonna thought. Suddenly his brow cleared, and he nodded. Maybe he'd just decided how much she was worth. She was unwillingly fascinated by the way his face changed moment-to-moment, like Long Island weather, and stared back, figuring she could be as rude as he was.

Her sweet southern mother would have urged her to lower her eyes, since men didn't like bold girls, but it had been a long time since Rhonna had taken her mother's cautious advice. Two years ago her mother had died, fading away into silence, and Rhonna felt guilty sometimes that she had not at least pretended to listen. Her mother used to warn plaintively that if men didn't think you were a lady, they would treat you like a tramp. Since Rhonna had been a Promise Keeper from the age of fourteen, she didn't need to be warned about letting interested males get too close. *Mother too often thought being a proper lady was the same as being a good Christian*, Rhonna said to herself. The only thing that stuck from her mother's instructions was a belief Rhonna shared with most of the other country kids that had grown up on Long Island's South Fork. They all agreed that you'd be a fool to trust the city slickers who were grabbing all the farmland and putting up garish mansions that would embarrass even Beverly Hills. If the beach was being ruined and the tap water turning to salt, it was because of the summer people and the developers, who were morphing Southampton into a country version of Manhattan's upper East Side.

Especially, the local folks all believed, you couldn't trust the men. They ate fresh-faced neighborhood girls for breakfast, lunch and dinner, the way they did the local steamed clams. You couldn't even get clams for under twenty dollars a pound anymore, because all the New York City people bought them up for their clambakes on the beach with their guests, famous and infamous, all people who didn't care squat about the land. Rhonna had a secret cove on her small, private beachfront strip where she could still dig clams and dance to the music of the waves, but she expected that some arrogant Manhattanite would raid her treasures one of these days. She had heard such people laughing at the Southampton natives, calling them potato heads with zits. As everyone in town agreed, the mocking sophisticates weren't to be trusted. They drank, smoked, and took drugs at their loud outdoor parties. Her pastor had warned his teenagers to stay away from these people and for the most part, Rhonna had taken his advice.

The looks of the man who had set the terminal door spinning out of control were arresting, at least. You had to give him that, rude as he was. He wore the sort of casually elegant tan slacks and moss green sweater tied around his neck that marked the rich Southampton social set. Rhonna had seen the type before, too many times, but this one looked like he had set the trend, not followed it. His wiry, dark red hair was perfectly cut, but a cowlick made one lock fall down over his broad, tanned forehead. He wore a thick mustache that almost hid his wide, mobile mouth. Just now he was frowning in concentration, but for a moment, she had imagined how his face would look when he smiled. Rhonna shook her head, remembering how many suave, tall, jet set men like this one had tried to slip through her defenses and not made it.

The man was at her side in a moment, standing too close. Rhonna backed off a little, but he just took a step closer. Maybe he was a southern European, Rhonna thought. She had heard they maintained close contact, not letting the other person breathe. For some reason, she really was having trouble breathing, and she put her hand to her throat, resting her long pink nails on her skin, feeling the throb of blood just under the fingertips. He was too close, she thought, too much taller than she, too sure of himself for Rhonna not to feel a strong urge to turn her back and pretend he wasn't there. Yet she found herself looking up into his eyes, not moving, letting him merge his space with hers. The feeling wasn't altogether uncomfortable, but she found her body tightening in distress as she tried to sort out her mixed feelings.

"You'd do just fine, except for that cute little cleft in your chin. About five six, 110 pounds, right?" His voice was crisp and businesslike, as if he were closing a deal.

"Right, but wrong. *If there's a deal being cut here*, Rhonna thought, *I sure want to be in on it.* "Hey, I don't even know who you are."

"Cal Conway," the man said, waiting for her to recognize the name, which she did, with a sinking heart. Cal Conway was the best environmental journalist in the country, maybe the world. He had won the Pulitzer just last year for his story on the Amazon rain forests. Now governments all over the world were paying their people to plant trees and taxing them for cutting trees down. The man was making a difference. Maybe her grandchildren would someday be able to breathe without gas masks, her father had commented at the time, because of this man's reporting. But her father had also wondered how long Cal Conway would be alive to do his work. He had been responsible for getting a lot of do-nothings in the Department of the Interior fired, and done a lot of developers out of deals. Studying Conway's craggy face, Rhonna felt a sudden chill run through her body as she imagined his loss. He might be a tough, arrogant egotist, she thought, but he was effective, and he was on the right side.

Somewhere Rhonna had read that Cal Conway's wealthy family had disowned him for revealing some nasty little secrets. Corporate friends of theirs had tried to get government parkland for timber, and Cal Conway had let the world know about it. She vaguely remembered one of them, Ned Peavey, the inventor of corporate sleaze, according to Cal Conway. Her heart sank when she realized how little she understood the scene outside her little Long Island community. *Can I figure out how somebody like Cal Conway gets stories I couldn't hope to? Unless*...her mind worked fast, as it always had, for which she was grateful...*unless I can team up with him, maybe get some introductions, some inside information.*

But that would be sneaky, she told herself, and sneaky she had never been. Her right hand crept up to touch the cross around her neck. *Jesus, Lord, I ask you, don't let me turn into a sneak just because I need money.* It would be like trying to serve God and Mammon. There were stories she could have gotten, like the one on the real environmental costs of the new beachfront hotel in Southampton, if she had been willing to betray some of her childhood friends on the environmental impact board.

The whole idea of using people made her uncomfortable, which is why, practical Megan said, Rhonna never got ahead. Of course Megan had to use only fashion hints dropped by European buyers in her mother's store, while Rhonna would have had to stoop a whole lot lower. Too low, she thought, trying to size up Cal Conway's enigmatic expression. *I'm not going to lie,* she decided, *and I'm not going to steal somebody else's stuff.* But she didn't have to tell him she knew who he was. *Keeping quiet isn't lying, after all,* she reminded herself, hoping God would forgive her for this lapse in principles. Rhonna gave Cal Conway a slight, noncommittal nod, as if she knew little about him and didn't think much of what she knew.

"I'm asking you to come with me to Malta," Cal Conway said in his level bass voice, glancing quickly at his watch. "We'll have to hurry. They're boarding first class now."

"I'll get to Malta by myself, thanks," Rhonna said stiffly, shifting her heavy shoulder bag. "They told me there are still some economy class tickets left."

Just as she spoke, an attendant called out, "Only ticketed passengers in this line. No more tickets being sold."

Rhonna left her place in line and ran up to the desk, ignoring the annoyance on the face of the man first in line. "Look, my travel agent said this is a red-eye flight. There's always a seat left."

"Not this time, honey," the clerk said, giving her a friendly looking over as male functionaries always did. "Paris in the springtime, y'know."

"I'm just stopping in Paris on my way to Malta," she said, a catch in her voice warning her that tears weren't far off. "Can't you find me another flight? I'll go via Uganda if I have to."

The clerk shrugged and went on stamping documents for the couple who were edging Rhonna off to the side. She let her shoulder bag fall to the floor and stood clenching her fists, willing the tears not to come. This job would have earned her at least ten thousand dollars. Two years' worth of back taxes on the farm. She felt her stomach contract at the thought of losing the house and thirty acres where her family had lived for a hundred years, since they had emigrated from Northern Ireland. They had done the only thing they knew how to do, farm potatoes and done fine, too, until the rich people started buying up all the Southampton land, and property taxes went over the top. Rhonna's family farm was one of the few left, and it wouldn't be left for long if some money didn't drop out of the sky. She had run out of ways to make it happen.

A deep voice spoke next to her ear, and Rhonna lookedup into Cal Conway's face. "You've got it all wrong. This isn't a proposition, just business. I need a secretary fast, somebody who looks like the one I just lost to a bad case of mumps. Your face is enough like hers not to wig out the passport people. Wear her Foster Grants and you'll get by. Her passport will give you a free ticket and a seat in first class. You game?" He handed her a pair of glasses, which she held out stiffly in front of her, so he wouldn't think he had scored.

"What do I have to do?" Rhonna spoke slowly, needing a little time. If only he weren't standing so close that she could smell his fresh, warm breath as he spoke. Strange, how she couldn't remember noticing the smell of a man's breath before, except when it was bad. This one made her suspect he would taste good. *Cut it out, Rhonna,* she thought, mentally slapping herself on the cheek.

You're not going to kiss this guy, just maybe be his secretary for a couple of days. What do you care how he tastes?

"Show up for a few hours each day, is all. Take some notes and type them. You do type, yes?"

"Yes," she said sullenly. She was a virtuoso typist, having been a writer since she was seven. She was a Van Cliburn among typists, and even typed to soft Christian rock, keeping the beat. But she didn't like the idea of doing this man's typing for him when he was writing the stories she wanted to write. Still, a free ticket was a major incentive to eat her pride. Maybe he was an answer to prayer.

"What do you have there, an iPad?" Rhonna tried to keep her tone objective. "I can use one."

"Good. This is going to be easy," Cal Conway said, looking her over through half closed, calculating eyes. Clearly, he had been using the silences between them to imagine what she would taste like, too, and to figure how he could get more for his money. A bargain-hunter, like all the other rich folks she'd run into.

"Don't bet on it," she said coolly, catching his drift. "Three hours a day, max, free tickets there and back, my own hotel room for a week. I'll do my thing for twenty-one hours a day and yours for three."

"And what, I wonder, will be your thing?" Cal Conway slung her bag over his shoulder and steered her toward the departure gate as skillfully as if he were guiding her across a dance floor. "Why are you trying to get to Malta?"

She started to answer truthfully, but stopped herself. This successful man would look down on her if he knew she were such a pitiful journalist that she needed to take his offer in order to get to her assignment. Already he had several times looked down at her out of the corners of his eyes as if checking her out, though not wanting her to notice.

"I have my reasons," she finally said. "You wouldn't be interested."

"Try me," he said, giving their tickets to the clerk, and putting their luggage on the security belt. They waited together at the other side. She could feel his body next to hers, closer than she would like, but the line was crowded. He might not have meant to shove his hard, long leg up against hers as he reached down to pick up the bags. Rhonna wanted to edge away, embarrassed at the way her cheeks heated up at the touch of him, as if there were no fabric between his skin and hers. She stood very still instead, trying to breathe deeply and calm down, thinking that it was the overseas travel that was exciting her, something she had always wanted to do and was finally getting her chance. *Anyone would be nervous,* she told herself, whether or not they were with a hunk whose dark eyes drew hers like a magnet.

A heavy, bearded man lunged at the conveyer belt to drop off a suitcase as thick as he was. Rhonna fell against the railing, twisting her ankle, but before she went down, Cal Conway had an arm around her, pulling her even closer to him than she had been before. She smelled the bracing, piney aroma of his aftershave and her face rubbed against the arm of his dark green cashmere sweater. She heard his heart, racing like hers, and when she turned her face up, she saw that his had flushed dark and that a little muscle beside his mouth was working. For a moment she could not move, her legs trembled so, and something in her body seemed to be melting, softening her right up to her moistened, parted lips.

"You all right?" He set her firmly on her feet, looking into her eyes so intently that she could see her own reflected in his. "Can't imagine you take many falls, the way you walk. Like a dancer."

"I just twisted my ankle." Rhonna's voice sounded strange to herself, husky and uncertain. She would not let him see how his touch had stirred her, and she straightened up, pulling away from his hands. He was not a man who would need much encouragement for a closer than professional relationship during the coming week.

Best to let him think he had zero to hope for. She had promises to keep, and none of them could be to a man like him.

"Nothing a six-hour rest on the plane won't take care of." This time her voice was cool and clear.

Hearing the aloofness in her tone, Cal Conway turned his back on her, clearing a path so she could follow in his wake toward the waiting plane. The heavy, black-bearded man was in front of them all the way, turning back momentarily to nod and speak to Cal, who answered brusquely.

"Who is that?" she finally asked, getting close enough to him for him to hear her whisper. "His face looks familiar."

"You've probably seen him in *People Magazine* with one of his movie star girl friends," Cal said between gritted teeth. "Ned Peavey. Owns half the mineral interests in Canada and plenty in the U.S. too. Why am I not surprised he'll be at the conference?"

"Because he'd like to sabotage it," Rhonna said without thinking, remembering all she had read about Peavey's deals to swing government natural resource policy in his favor. "Because he'd like to get the mineral rights under the rain forests when they've been clear cut."

"You know about that?" Cal whirled around and stared at her, stopping the line for a moment. "You've been reading more than *People Magazine*, Miss Moran."

"Rhonna. And we're holding up the line." She gave him a little shove, then pulled her hands away as if they had touched an electric wire. Any contact with his body seemed to shake her as if she was a leaf in a storm. *Is it because he knows so much? Because he has the power I want myself?* It would take her some time to sort out just what she felt about Cal Conway, Rhonna thought, brushing back a lock of blond hair behind her ear. Competitive men like him always made her mad. They had too much of an edge, because unlike her, they had no feelings, at least none that she could see. Just ran over everybody else as if the soft ones like herself, who cared and tried to do the decent thing, were so many potatoes in the dirt.

Maybe that was one of the reasons she hadn't ever been tempted by any of the men who had tried to pressure her into an affair. Either they were too soft, like poor, poisoned Stan, or they were too tough and selfish, like Cal Conway probably was. Besides, as a Promise Keeper, she had made a vow not to make love until she was married, which was the main reason she was still a virgin at twenty-three.

She would pretend to sleep on the plane, she decided, though it would be hard, with this man's long, lean form stretched out beside her in the luxurious first class seats the flight attendant was settling them into. He would want to ask her what she knew about the conference, about the people there who were, like Ned Peavey, trying to turn its results to their own ends. And he would look into her face with that piercing gaze, trying to draw her into the brown depths of his eyes, and maybe succeeding at making her tell the truth. He was first of all, a world-class journalist, the kind Megan had improbably hoped to make of her, a man used to getting what he wanted out of people.

Well, thought Rhonna, turning down the bubbling glass of champagne the flight attendant tried to push into her hand, *Mr. Cal Conway won't get anything out of me.* As far as he knew, she was just a potato farmer's daughter out for a holiday. She had to smile, thinking that wasn't so far from the truth.

"You have a way of smiling," Cal Conway said to her, stirring the dry martini he had ordered instead of champagne, "that makes me think of a wicked, charming little girl who is about to put her brother's pet turtle back in the pond. Surface sweetness, but an iron will. Do I read you right, Rhonna Moran?"

When he turned to speak to her, his hand brushed hers, as if by accident. Since this man was in thorough control of his life, Rhonna doubted that much happened to him by accident. Probably anything that happened to her while she was with him was not by accident either. It bothered her that such a man could manipulate her and events as he pleased, even though she felt also a sense of calm relief, as if she could, at any time, let him take the wheel of her life and be sure she wouldn't crash. Such men were dangerous, Rhonna reflected, because they made giving up her power so easy, so desirable. She would have to be on guard, to be sure she didn't sink into the kind of childlike trust that might give him the control over her mind that he already had over her feelings.

"Actually, I did put my cousin's pet turtle back in the pond, when I was eight." She kept the conversation light, not letting her rapid pulse tease her into the depths. "Funny you should have guessed. He had forgotten to feed it, and the poor thing was dying. I'm pretty nuts over animals. Can't stand to see them suffer. When an oil slick hit our beach, I was just a little kid, but I ran all over the place trying to rescue water birds, crying my face off. Spent all night trying to wipe away the oil and all day burying the ones that died."

She felt tears come to her eyes, remembering that terrible day, and sniffed, feeling stupid and sentimental in front of this worldly man. She had not meant to reveal any confidences to him, and here she was, telling him what was at the core of her heart. He would probably laugh at her, Rhonna thought, futilely rifling through her purse for a tissue.

Cal Conway took his neatly folded cocktail napkin and expertly, tenderly, wiped the corners of her eyes. "I felt the same way," he said. "I was at the family's Shelter Island beach house when the slick hit. My sister and I took pictures for the newspapers and rounded up sick birds to take to our zoo's rehab center. I had this idea that if people just saw how the wildlife was suffering, they'd do something about the men who were causing the trouble."

"And did they? Did you make your point?" She tried to remind herself not to relax, not to be taken in by Cal's seeming kindness. In his line of work, he had probably learned to be a good actor.

"I got the pictures published and a story with them, in the *Daily News*, which was quite a coup for a 16-year-old," Cal said, his voice hard and remote, as if he were back there when the oil slick turned the South Fork beaches deadly. "The story started me on my career, but it did nothing to change the way men like Ned Peavey trash the environment. You know what I think?"

"Can't even guess." Rhonna felt giddy, her heart pounding as the plane sped down the runway. She wondered if it was from excitement at the take-off or at Cal's talking from the heart. *Maybe he talks that way to everybody*, she said to herself, trying to breathe deeply and restore her calm. *Maybe I just think we're making a connection. I've seen his type before, the type that gets to know women easily and dumps them just as easily.*

He responded as if he had guessed what she was thinking. "The men who're turning our environment into sludge are exactly the men who use women any way they want. Funny, how the two things go together. Why might that be?"

Rhonna felt a sudden lightness and her heart danced as the plane lifted off the ground. He understood her fears without her having to tell him, and was letting her know where he stood. It was as if she and this stranger were on a cloud, alone in a great, wide space, where they could speak the same language, touch, and meet. It was as if he could read her mind, knew what she feared, what she loved. For a moment her distrust fell away and she looked into his eyes as fearlessly and openly as if she had been talking to her father.

"It's power, isn't it? Using and controlling. I've always been afraid of that in a man, unless he's a Christian."

The words slipped out before she realized what she was saying, before she realized she was saying something that was true of her and this warm, strong masculine presence that pulled her inexorably into his orbit like a massive star. For reassurance, she reached up and touched the gold cross around her neck and noticed that Cal's eyes followed her move.

"I haven't been one for a long time," he said, his voice sounding remote and a little sad. When she shivered a little, he laid a blanket over her, and tucked it around her shoulders, sending that now familiar electric thrill deep into her body. "But I remember my Christian mother saying that power can be used for good as well as evil. Remember that, Rhonna Moran, and don't mistake one for the other."

"I wish I had the power to save my father's land from the tax collector," she murmured, "That's all the power I want. To keep our little beach off Dune Road just the way it's always been."

"I've seen that beach," Cal said softly, his lips close to her ear, "and I agree with you."

"I hope you know how to stop them," Rhonna said, holding her hands together tightly to keep them from trembling. His breath seemed to move right through her, like wind through a tree. She tried to keep her tone cool and objective, hoping not to sound as rattled as she felt. "Men like Ned Peavey, I mean."

"I think I do. But it's not the time to talk about it." He settled back into his seat, as if by putting a little distance between them, he wouldn't be tempted to tell any secrets. "Will you totally lose it if you have a glass of champagne?"

The flight attendant was coming by again, offering more to drink. Instead, Rhonna opted for a magazine, and leafed through it sleepily, aware that Cal Conway was still sipping his martini and watching her reflection in the windowpane beside him. The magazine had too many pictures of society people jet-setting to exotic destinations, and Rhonna, turned off, flipped through hastily, wondering why anyone would care what the Duchess of Kent had for breakfast on the island of Capri.

Suddenly her eyes opened wide, for there on the page was Cal Conway with a gorgeous brunette, an Italian countess the caption said, a woman whose wide-neckline black sweater was sliding off her shapely tanned shoulders and whose body was stuck to his as if by Crazy Glue. They were waving at somebody seeing them off on a yacht, and the caption said, *Two Beautiful People Doing the Blue Grotto.* Cal had his arm around her and was smiling as he lazed against the yacht rail.

So, Cal Conway was no less a user of women than Ned Peavey, she thought, laying the magazine open in his lap, and turning her face away to sleep. *He talks a better game, is all. He can have his countess. They deserve each other.* She had glanced at enough of the article to know that Countess Cristina had the moral integrity of a goat. As for Cal, what kind of man would want a woman who had been in the Italian law courts half a dozen times for shady dealings with the mafia? Rhonna had an obscure memory of seeing the countess's picture with Ned Peavey in *Newstar.* They had been frolicking at Baron's Cove resort, where the rich and famous went to show off their jewelry and their cars. *If Cal wants women like Cristina*, Rhonna thought, *Lord knows he would be disappointed in a country girl like me.* And she would certainly be disappointed in him. *Better not to let him get any closer.* When Cal tried to start another conversation, she pretended she was asleep, leaving him to guess what she thought of his high-minded twaddle about how to treat women.

Her first guess had apparently been right. He was no more than the usual powerful, jet-set operator who enjoyed his game with women and played it by his own rules. She would stay well away from him when they got to Malta, except for her contracted three hours. In fact, she would try to spend some time with this Ned Peavey. With his history of womanizing, she could probably get more out of him than Cal Conway could, a thought which made her smile as she drifted off to sleep, listening to the drone of the engines that made her body throb with a vague, unrecognizable longing.

Rhonna awoke just as they were being told to straighten their seats for landing. She tried not to look out the window, not to let Cal Conway know she had never before seen Paris, but her heart leaped at a glimpse of a soaring steel tower in the distance as the plane dipped, and a light-framed arch with tiny cars circling around it. Buildings that glowed ghostly white were surrounded by rich green parks that were strung with jewel-like lanterns. Never before had Rhonna seen a place where what was manmade was as beautiful as nature. Her lips parted and she sighed her pleasure. Beauty would be her undoing, she thought, sinking into this vision of light and marble. *I'm a fool for beauty and always have been*, Rhonna told herself, trying not to betray the intensity of her feeling. That was why she needed to watch out for Cal. If ever a man had struck her as beautiful, it was this one.

For Rhonna, beauty meant wildness, freedom, power, not just pleasing features. That was why she liked to look at Cal's craggy hawk-nose and thick, alive auburn hair, and that was precisely why she should not let her looks linger, why she must not let him into the dreamscape of her imagination. There she had always longed to find a Christian man who wanted to share his soul with her, not just his body. This Cal Conway was definitely not that man.

Cal followed her gaze, and smiled when she blushed and pretended to be more interested in putting on her lipstick than in the view. "You don't have to play the jaded world traveler with me," he mocked, leaning back so she could see better. "The City of Light deserves your attention from every angle. There's no more beautiful sight on God's earth. Except maybe Victoria Falls when you fly through the spray in a small plane. Or the Amazon delta under a full moon." His eyes looked into the distance, and he smiled for a moment, a smile that vanished into his mustache quickly, as if he preferred not to let her know what sights had touched and opened his heart.

How many things he has seen, she thought, feeling suddenly small and ignorant. What would it take for her to follow this same path, see what he had seen and turn it into words that would move people to cherish and protect the Lord's fragile, lovely earth so it could grow three hundred foot trees and strong children and good, healthy potatoes? Rhonna felt a sudden sense of helplessness and sorrow. She felt as she had in childhood when garbage washed up on their beach, and no plastic bag seemed big enough to hold it all. The task was so big and she knew so little, had so few contacts, was going on nothing but nerve and prayer.

The plane banked and dipped, so that she could see the wing extending to the right, its red light blinking as the landing gear thudded down into place. Rhonna pressed her nose to the window and stared, her heart beating fast. Her travel dreams had always been of jungles and mountain lakes, but here was something else, undreamed of and alien, like landing on another planet. The lights of Paris wrapped around domes and towers. Their reflection shimmered like diamonds in the River Seine, snaking through the city, lapping at churches full of windows that exclaimed light.

"It looks like a giant chandelier, doesn't it?" Cal Conway's voice was soft and faraway. "Paris is where the night is a time for being awake. Too good to sleep through. When I'm in Paris I hardly sleep at all. The energy of the place keeps me high. How'd you like to stay up all night and see Paris?" He turned around and faced her, his eyes brilliant and piercing, as if he meant to hypnotize her into saying yes.

Rhonna was immediately on her guard. He probably had a little pad somewhere on the Left Bank, where he'd steer a woman to after introducing her to the delights of a Montmartre floor show and a carafe of absinthe. She had almost fallen into the arms of such a man back home in D'Antonio's Trattoria, after drinking her first and last vodka martini. Like Cal, that man was the type who would have made the most of any weakness. Good thing Bill Kingsley had come on the scene, sent the slick city guy on his way, and driven her home.

Rhonna's mind felt better when it was clear, so that she could feel whatever was going on, not just let it pass by her. People who walked the beach with earphones and taped music baffled her. Rhonna wanted nothing between her and what was real, nothing that could blur her senses or control her feelings. She liked having her mind clear so she could feel God's presence in the world around her. *Who needs cigarettes when you could just breathe pure, simple air? There's so much to feel*, she thought, *so much that escapes most people. No wonder they need to get drunk or high.* As for her, just the feel of wet moss against her bare feet when she walked in the farm's pebbly creek made her breathless with bliss. An easy turn-on, Bill Kingsley said she was, and warned her, in his fatherly way, that she'd better be careful with men. The wrong kind would have an antenna for that sensual gift of hers. Bill hadn't needed to tell her. She had known from her early years that she was too vulnerable to be careless.

"I like to walk," she said cautiously. "No drinks, no discos, no nightclubs. But if you want to show me something I can see from the street, okay."

Cal was patient, seeming to understand she had her reasons for being suspicious. He ticked off the facts, like the reporter he was. "We have six hours before we leave for Malta. Too long to spend in the airport. How about it? Up to walking in the rain?"

"I love walking in the rain. Or in fog, the kind that rolls in over the beach at home. The kind that seems to sink into you until you're part of it."

She closed her eyes for a moment, and remembered the feeling, how the arms of the fog enfolded her like a lover's, leaving moisture all over her and a sense that she and the fog were one and the same. Moments like that were a kind of prayer, and Rhonna thanked God for them.

Cal's deep voice seemed to come from far away, though she could feel his breath on her cheek, he was so close. "I wish I knew what was going on in your head when you close your eyes and get that soft look on your face, like somebody just fed you a mouthful of whipped cream. Any man would give a lot to be responsible for such a look."

Rhonna's eyes flew open. She was embarrassed, as if caught by a stranger in some intimate act. "We were talking about Paris in the rain," she said shortly. "Not me."

Cal put on his tweed jacket and smoothed his tousled auburn hair with both hands. "Okay, Paris. It's always raining at night in Paris if it's spring. Not real rain, just a sort of damp that hangs in the air and smells like fish or sweet jasmine, depending on how close to the Seine you are. Yes? You'll come?" He turned to her suddenly, just as the plane touched the ground, and the thud in her heart matched the pounding of the wheels touching the tarmac.

"I'd like to see Paris any way I can," Rhonna faltered, suddenly not caring if he knew she was an ignorant country girl who had never been anywhere. "In the rain, at night, would be fine."

She was sleepy, and her head was spinning with jet lag. She didn't know if she could walk the city streets for six hours or hold off this insistent man, obsessed as he was with the beauty of this place he loved. *Lord be with me. Keep me awake to your presence in this gorgeous place with this gorgeous man.* She was taking a risk, but at least she knew it. Rhonna's back straightened as she slung her carry-on over her shoulder and followed the other first class passengers. Ned Peavey turned to stare at her, his small, dark, glittering eyes communicating interest, but she looked away. Perhaps later she would speak to him, find out what he knew. At least, with all that staring, he was likely to remember her face. Right now she was in the mood for Paris at night. Information and maneuvering to know what she needed to know would come later.

"Où est la consigne?" Cal said briskly to the customs man who quickly waved them through and pointed toward a door on their left. First class tickets gave you an advantage, Rhonna observed. Nobody at customs bothered to open your bags, and you were the first ones through the line. Despite her one year of French in school, she wasn't sure what a *consigne* was until Cal took her bag from her shoulder. He shoved her passport into his inside pocket, with his own, and dropped off their hand luggage with the first-class lounge clerk who seemed to know Cal's name and brightened up, as if expecting a big tip, which he got. Cal kept euros in one back pocket and dollars in another, ready for anything, she thought, wondering if that was what a person needed to make it as a journalist. She was too sleepy to be ready for anything but bed, though Cal Conway was going to be the last person to know that.

A taxi took them straight into Paris, right to the Pont Neuf, where Cal said their tour would begin. Not knowing much French, Rhonna wasn't sure where they were going, but at least it wasn't a hotel. She knew enough to be sure that hotel was hotel in any language. The Pont which turned out to be a bridge, was hundreds of years old and looked like it would stand another thousand years. It was tough, sturdy, and yet graceful. Rhonna found herself wanting to climb it like a mountain, finding footholds in the little holes where plants had sprung up.

She had a great love for old things, especially for old things made of rock. They reminded her of the agelessness of the rocks by the beach at home and of European churches which had stood through everything from Viking raids to German bombs, steady as the faith that built them. Rocks gave her a feeling of security and honesty. *They've been there longer than human beings*, Rhonna thought, and had gotten over any stupid notions of taking charge or abusing what was not as strong as they were. *Sometimes God must be a lot more pleased with rocks than with us humans.* Rhonna reached over and touched the pocked, ancient stone of the bridge, caressing the holes lightly.

"It's suffering from pollution," she said softly. "Too many fumes. I hate to think of how even stone crumbles in bad air."

"It's happening all over Europe," Cal said. "Which doesn't make the the pocks in the Pont Neuf any easier to accept." He took her elbow. "We'll go down the stairs here. I want you to smell the good, honest stink of ancient water. Do you mind not having an umbrella?" He pushed her loose tendrils of hair behind her ears, as if aware that most women would not be happy to have their make-up melting and their hair turning to overcooked macaroni in this insistent drizzle.

Since Rhonna wore no makeup but a light lipstick, which had long since worn off, and her hair turned alive and shining with rain, she wanted no umbrella. The night was warm and gentle. All she could think of was that Cal Conway's arm was tight around her waist, keeping her from stumbling on the irregular steps. She loved the taste of the sweet rain on her mouth and let her lips part, holding her head back, so the rain could run into her mouth like kisses. Since Cal was keeping her on course, Rhonna could give herself totally to the rain, not looking at the pavement.

They paused at the bottom of the steps, where the river met the old stone parapet. Cal bent over her, his eyes searching her face, his mustache brushing her parted lips. "You belong in the rain," he said, his voice catching as if he had forgotten how to talk. "I love the way you catch the rain in your mouth."

Before she could move away, his arms were around her and his body leaned into hers. For a moment she let her mouth open, receiving him like the rain, like the moist rich air of this city of light and mystery. For this moment he was the longed-for, faraway place, the one that reminded her of all she never had and always wanted. He felt like part of her, so much so that she could feel the rippling currents of energy pouring from her fingers into his body and streaming through it as that same power was streaming through her own.

If she didn't stop now, Rhonna thought, she would be unable to stop. Already she was feeling a strange melting sensation in her legs that made it almost impossible to stand up. If he had not been holding her, she would have fallen. *Terrifying,* she thought, *to depend so utterly on someone, on this man you hardly know, but who has known and thrown away so many women. A man to whom I am only a convenient warm body on a rainy night in Paris.* Suddenly Rhonna felt strength surge through her. *Lord, I know you expect more of me than this. Help me fight this temptation. If I don't resist now,* she thought, *I'll never make it through the week without letting this man do anything he wants with me.*

She pushed Cal away, so hard that he staggered, then quickly found his footing, balanced and lithe as a cat. "Look, I'm not an easy mark and you're not Paris," she said, her voice shaking in her throat. "Let's go back to the airport. I need to sleep off the jet lag, this mist, this place that makes me want to cry and melt and be somebody else. The kiss too. Especially that."

"Rhonna," Cal said softly, reaching for her. "This could be a good night. Our night. A little trust would help. . ."

"No." She was running up the stone steps, stumbling a little, but knowing she would soon be up there with the cars and lights and streets full of people. "I'm going back to the airport. We have four hours and I have a book about the Maltese temples that will take me exactly that long to read. See you at the departure gate."

He did not follow her closely, just kept her in sight until she got into a taxi. What he did after that she had no idea, but all the way to the airport, she tasted his mouth against hers and wondered what else she would have seen in the cool fog of the Paris night if she had not feared that Cal Conway would sweep her away into some large, mysterious world of his own which she could understand little and control less.

Hardly looking at the scenes of Paris as the taxi passed them by, Rhonna prayed for strength. She knew she was being tested and that her decisions mattered to her future and even more, to her faith. How many times had she promised not even to date a man who wasn't a Christian, let alone kiss him? *Too many times to give in now,* she said to herself firmly, hoping she could be just as firm when Cal was nearby.

Rhonna slept all the way to Malta, her blanket pulled up under her chin and did not know that Cal spent the hours tossing next to her, often staring at her delicate profile and slightly opened lips, frowning a little, as if trying to memorize her face. He had the haunting feeling that he had seen her before, perhaps in a dream, and that she was carrying some secret about himself that he needed to know but had ignored. His mother had always said that he didn't know himself, but he had put that insight aside, along with whatever it was that had been lost with his childhood innocence. That had gone the way of her unanswered prayers for him to grow up into God. It occurred to him that this woman sleeping beside him still had what he had left behind, and he wanted to probe her lips, her slender body, for some hint of what had once been himself. *Tell the truth*, Cal said to himself with a tight smile, *I'd like to take her to bed. That's all it is.* Yet he still found himself staring and wondering why he wanted to protect her and take her for his own physical pleasure, at the same time. The paradox was an unfamiliar one, and its strangeness made him uneasy.

As her body stirred under the blanket and her face turned on the pillow until he could see only her profile, Cal felt a sudden flash of memory move him. He set his glass down on the tray because his hand shook for an instant. Once before, he had seen her. She had been wearing a flesh-pink bathing suit, dancing all by herself in the sunlight on a private, rock-rimmed beach, her hair in one long braid that hung to her waist. She had been only about fifteen, her body slight and supple as she bent and swayed in the sunlight that touched the unbound tendrils of her hair and turned them to a haze of gold around her face. He had been gathering samples of polluted ocean water, and had come up against a rock barrier that blocked his way. After climbing the rock wall, he had looked down into the cove and seen this girl-woman digging her toes into the sand as she danced, flinging her arms up to the sun, then back like wings. She had looked strong and graceful as a falcon about to take off. At the time he had wanted to call to her, even more to climb down to the stand and touch her, assuring himself she was real. But he had a sense then, as he did now, that she would not want to be intruded on.

Cal saw that the blanket was creeping up over her face, making her stir restlessly, and he tucked it back under her chin, letting his finger rest for a moment against the slight cleft that he felt a sudden longing to touch with his lips. When she turned her face toward him, he saw that the pink tip of her tongue had suddenly touched her upper lip like a petal, and his body tensed with a lightning current of longing. Even in her sleep she responded to his nearness. He wanted to run his hands over her neck and shoulders, pull her against him in the half darkness, and become part of whatever dream made her mouth so moist and soft.

Instead, he lay back and stared out the window at the lights of the French Riviera where they edged the Mediterranean shore. He would like to show Rhonna Moran the little town of Arles, Cal Conway thought, imagining her full lips parting wide at the sight of the ruined Greek theater columns standing against the flawlessly blue southern French sky, so like her eyes. *It's too bad*, he thought, *that she seems to have such a fear of me*. No, fear was not the word. This woman was not afraid of anything. What she seemed to be feeling was suspicion, and a sense that he would treat her as he had so many others. But none of them had gone straight to his heart as this one had the first time their eyes had met.

He sighed, lay back, and closed his eyes resolutely. It would be hard to keep his mind on what he had to do in Malta, given the presence of this blond, soft-voiced woman at his side, but the stakes were too high for him to let himself be distracted. With any luck he would blow wide open Ned Peavey's attempt to take over a Northeast timber reserve and the minerals lying under it. It might just be possible to leave some of the natural world intact for the next generation. Not his children, but someone else's, anyway. Maybe his own children too, he said to himself, wondering why he'd never thought about having children before. He took a last quick look at Rhonna's lips, half-smiling in sleep, then relaxed into a fitful sleep himself. The plane banked away from Italy and turned south toward the tiny island on which the environmentalists of the world would have their eyes trained for the next week.

Chapter Two

"This has got to be the hottest place I was ever in," Rhonna gasped. The overheated wind from Libya, two hundred miles south of Malta, hit her in the face as she got out of the plane. "It must be 105 out here."

"Be grateful it's the dry season," Cal said, leading the way down the metal staircase that burned through the soles of their shoes. "You wouldn't believe what Malta's like when it's humid. All a man can do is lie around in his hotel room with a wet towel over his bare skin."

"No air-conditioning?" Rhonna spoke fast, trying not to envision Cal Conway lying in bed with a wet towel shaping his lean body.

"Only in a few hotels." Cal took her elbow and guided her into the customs line. "Ours is one of them, thank God."

"You've been here before?" Rhonna wondered if there was anywhere this man had not been. Until Bill Kingsley had given her the assignment, she had barely known Malta existed.

"Once, overnight." Cal lifted his black leather bag onto the counter. "With a friend."

That would be the countess, Rhonna said to herself, setting her bag beside his. Cristina Montani, with the sweater that wouldn't stay on her shoulders and the mafia connection that was making her rich enough to buy whatever she wanted, no doubt including Cal Conway. The two of them probably couldn't survive without air-conditioning and cold buckets of champagne in their bedroom. She kept her tone dispassionate, despite her thoughts. "Then you don't speak Maltese?"

The customs man waved them along, not opening their bags, and Cal pointed to the auto rental desk. "Nobody speaks Maltese unless he was born here. You wouldn't believe what happens to a Romance language when Turkish gets mixed up with it. Luckily they all know English or Italian."

Rhonna kept silent, thinking that in this alien place, with this stranger who could turn her into a stranger to herself, she was as mixed up as the language. *As long as I'm here,* she thought, *I'd better be on my guard.* Cal Conway was the only person she knew here, and she didn't really know him. She knew only that the feeling of his body near her made her want two paradoxical things—to get away, and to get closer. Neither one suited her. Rhonna fanned her face with her straw hat and felt her heart pound. She hoped it was not fear, only the heat, but could not be sure.

The odd feeling persisted that somehow, in the night on the plane, Cal had touched her, taken some essential part of her as his own, and would not give it up. It was as if she had been violated in her sleep, but with some piece of her assenting to being taken, something in the core of her having been glad to belong to this man. *Well*, Rhonna thought, standing straighter, her hand at her throat to control the pounding pulse she felt there, *when I'm awake, I'm my own person, God's person. And that's how I'm going to stay until I'm safely home. I'm not chocolate, to melt in the hands of this man, just because it's hot, and I'm confused. Strange, how I've never felt so overcooked before, so soft, so. . .* she ran out of words and breath at the same time, and found herself suddenly dizzy.

"You're hyperventilating," Cal said, putting a strong arm around her, almost lifting her off the ground. "It happens here, in this heat. Here, sit on the bench. You need the shade. Put your head down." He sat with her until her breathing was normal again, pulling her against him as if willing her to connect with and copy his steady, even breaths. "Now, just wait for me here. I'll be back with the car. Don't try to walk around."

Cal rented a car for the week, explaining to her that they would need it to explore the island. The cost of a taxi for one day was the cost of a car rental for a week. Rhonna had wondered why the fleet of empty cabs had stood at the airport, waiting for their impossible fares, instead of meeting the market price. Maltese men must be either tough or stupid, she thought. Probably both. She caught their glances as she walked, feeling them start around the thighs and work upward, the way the glances of New York City men went. Feet and faces seemed to be equally uninteresting to such men. They had their own agenda, and a woman's mobility and identity were not part of it. *Will I ever find a man who values me for who I am?* She sighed. *Probably not, unless he was trying to live by God's law, not his own.*

The island was smaller than she had imagined, and ten minutes after leaving Luqa Airport, she and Cal were pulling into the capital of Malta. The port city of Valletta looked something like what Paris might have looked in the nineteenth century. Rhonna gazed at the narrow streets with their old, charming stores, and balconied, ivory-colored buildings, looking slightly the worse for wear and leaning inward over the cobblestoned alleys. Their hotel was the best one in Valletta, Cal told Rhonna. The building was old but elegant, and near both downtown and the great arched gateway where tourists found buses that would take them all over the island. Their hotel was next to the harbor, with tall windows and balconies big enough only for a bistro table and two chairs.

"I thought we were just going to be together for three hours in the morning, at the conference," Rhonna said suspiciously, as the hotel clerk took them up to their rooms in the rickety elevator, looking at her midsection as intently as the cab drivers at the airport had. Perhaps that was because Maltese women over the age of eighteen seemed to have massive bellies and hips. Megan would have looked like a mere shadow of a woman next to these, Rhonna said, smiling to herself and thinking she must tell Megan to vacation here sometime. The older women who were lugging groceries or cleaning the streets were loud, heavy, and strong as the ten-foot high stone goddesses that had once stood in the ancient temples. Strange, how the young Maltese girls looked like flowers in the wind, and yet their mothers turned into giant tree trunks, Rhonna thought. Something in the water, maybe. Or the fat might be their way of getting back at the men who ogled the slim foreign women and the short-skirted, giggling schoolgirls.

"A contract's a contract," she added, thinking that Cal Conway, with his jet-setting women, was no different in kind from the leering Maltese taxi drivers.

"That's up to you." Cal said shortly, catching the coldness in her voice. "I plan to see the temples of Malta, since I didn't have time when I was here last. Some of them are six thousand years old, older than the pyramids. You're invited, but suit yourself."

Rhonna didn't answer, not sure of what would suit her. She had not been prepared for this knock-out heat, for the sweat that made the navy blue tank top stick to her body like a second skin, and for the electric feel of Cal Conway's hands brushing against hers as the two of them walked down the red carpeted hotel hall. Besides, she knew enough about the temples already to be her own guide. The story of the old pagan goddesses saddened her. The people who had believed in them had disappeared without trace, eons before the Hebrews had brought the world their message of the One God. Now the Maltese worshipped Christ at Ta'Pinu, the church that had replaced the pagan temples. In the four hours at the airport, Rhonna realized, she had probably learned more about the Maltese nature goddesses and their gigantic burial halls than Cal Conway would ever care to know.

Cal's room was next door to hers, as she had feared, with a locked door between them. She tested the door, trying not to let him see what she was doing, but Cal Conway didn't seem to miss a move she made. One of his dark eyebrows, peaking at the center, rose in amusement as she tested the door. At least she thought it was amusement. From the grim look around his mouth, she couldn't be sure. Maybe his usual secretary, the girl with the mumps, left the door open when the two of them travelled together. More passed between the two rooms, she figured, than fast food and computer printouts. The thought of the open door during all the many nights the two must have spent in exotic, foreign hotels made Rhonna take in her breath sharply, so that Cal asked if she found anything wrong with the room.

"No," Rhonna said, walking to the window and pulling up the shade. "I like it. Something about these old, faded walls and the flowered bedspread makes me think of home."

Change was hard for her, she suddenly realized. Deep inside, she had a fear that all good things were doomed to come to a premature end, and that she would not be strong enough to bear their loss. That kind of strength was what she prayed for most, next to her father's life and saving their farm. *The farm is his life,* she thought, *and he can't survive losing it.* She mustn't think of that, Rhonna said resolutely to herself. *Stay in the moment. There, with the grace of God, I will be safe.*

She caught her breath again as she looked through the window and looked across the crooked streets and shops to see the harbor. Already she missed being at home and hearing the waves crashing on the rocks. Here, the sea was tame and predictable, not like the wild, thunderous surf on the shore of the South Fork.

"I'm glad you like it. Thought you'd prefer a place with atmosphere. Not everybody does." He tipped the bellboy and closed the door when the young man left. "When I crash in Paris, I stay in a place like this. It's got the feel I like. You can put your feet on the bed without the housekeeper expecting an extra tip for your lapse." He lay down on her bed, put his hands behind his head and crossed one ankle over the other. "You'll find this comfortable, I think. Hard. Your body doesn't look like you'd want a soft mattress."

Rhonna walked over to the window, not wanting him to see the flush that burned her cheeks when he mentioned her body. She also wanted to send a message that she would not be checking the comfort of the bed as long as he was in it.

"You have a place of your own in Paris?" She tried to keep her tone noncommittal, but felt a bitter rage rising in her like heartburn. Her guess had been right, then. She had done well to spend her first Parisian night in the safety of the airport.

"A place that's mine to use. Perk of A.P. foreign correspondents." She could hear the bed creak as he got up. Good. He wasn't going to stay there, expecting her to join him. "It's right next to the Paris Opera House. You'd like the view." He paused, and then added in a low voice. "And I'd like to show it to you. See it through fresh eyes. Yours."

Rhonna could feel his presence close behind her as she stood by the window, looking out at the walls built by crusaders and Turks in the days when Malta was a kingdom of pirates. Of men like Cal who needed a place to crash when they were resting up between raids, with women to help them relax, playing the only role such men thought they were good for.

"I'd like to get some sleep," she said, not turning around, not trusting herself to be face to face with him. "A little jet lag. Do you mind?"

"Not at all. I'll catch a bit myself before the conference convenes this afternoon. Pick you up at noon for lunch?" He kept his tone casual, but she could hear an edge to it, as if he were either angry or thinking ahead to the assignment that obviously meant more to him than just a story. Maybe he was remembering picking those oil-soaked birds off the shore when he was a boy, before he had lost his innocence. It had been a long time, she was sure, since this man had been innocent.

"Yes. You might brief me later on what you expect to happen." Rhonna did not follow him to the door, wanting to widen the distance between them. "I'll be of more use if I know what's going on."

He paused at the door, and she turned to look at him, wishing she could keep her eyes from tangling with his. "You know more than you let on, Rhonna Moran," he said, his voice light. "One of these days you'll tell me."

"Don't hold your breath." Rhonna made an effort to smile, but felt he was patronizing her, thinking her just a silly farm girl. Turning the lock when he was out the door, she had the strangest feeling. As she stood with her head against the door she felt that on the other side of it was Cal Conway not wanting to move away either. He was feeling what she was feeling, Rhonna was sure of it. But beyond the strange, twisting thrill that shot through her body and his, what did he feel, after all? *Certainly not the thrill of first love*, she smiled grimly, pulling off her soggy clothes. Certainly not the breathless sense she herself had of coming smack up against a mystery that drew her into a whirlpool of confusion and turned her brain dizzy as she tried to understand this man whose mind and body seemed in sync with hers like another self. She knew him, and she didn't know him. He was as she might have been, had she been a man, but completely alien. They might have some of the same feelings, Rhonna thought, but their experience was wholly different, opening an unbridgeable gulf between them. *It's like trying to mate a sea gull and an eagle,* she said to herself grimly. *And guess which one's the predator.*

Rhonna lay on the bed, stripped to her underwear, with damp towels lying over her as she tried to say a prayer before sleep. It was a good way to avoid anxiety nightmares, she had always found. The air-conditioning Cal had bragged about was not working, and the thick, hot Maltese air made her feel like she had suddenly gained thirty pounds. It was no wonder people here spent the two or three hottest hours in the day flat on their backs in the dark.

From time to time, she drifted into dreams in which Cal was rescuing her from heavy-lidded Maltese taxi drivers, with more on their minds than an over-priced fare. Each time, she woke up thinking she felt the scratch of his mustache against her face and smelled his piney scent, close as if he were lying beside her. She sniffed a little and poked at the pillow. It did smell a little like him, just from the few minutes he had lain on her bed. Probably Cal knew just what trace he was leaving behind, Rhonna thought, turning the pillow over in annoyance. He didn't miss a trick.

When the dreams wouldn't let her sleep anymore, she leafed through the illustrations in her book on the Maltese temples. They were built like thick-waisted figure eights, in the shape of a horizontal female bodies sprawled over the flat rocky countryside in vast disarray, like large, loose-limbed sleeping women. The earliest builders were perhaps trying to duplicate the caves they inhabited in the northern glacial wastes. Her eye was caught by a reference to the cave of Ghar Dalam, the earliest dwelling of the prehistoric Maltese. It was a half hour bus ride away. Anything that would take her out of range of Cal Conway's pervasive presence was fine with her. The idea of caves had always appealed to her. She imagined that it would be like going straight to the heart of mother earth and feeling nature as immediately as if God had just created it.

She threw on a pink cotton gauze float over a cotton slip that was damp as soon as it touched her skin, and eased out the door, hoping Cal wouldn't hear her leave. As she passed his door, she paused, fighting an absurd desire to lean her head against it so that she might hear him if he were up and moving. Of course he was sleeping in this heat, unaware of her. Probably he was dreaming of the black-haired countess and their adventures in the Blue Grotto. Rhonna walked passed the door fast, trying not to remember the magazine picture of the countess smiling toothily up into Cal's face.

When she got down to the first floor, she saw Ned Peavey in the lobby. He saw her, too, and stood up, tucking his expensive-looking silk shirt into his beige linen slacks. He was a large man, and obviously had to work overtime to keep his shirt from parting company with the top of his pants.

"Let me guess," he said, sauntering over to her. "You want to go touring before the conference. May I be your guide?"

"I'm headed for Ghar Dalam," she said, lowering her eyes as her mother had taught her. This was a man who begged for insincerity. "If you want to drive me, fine."

A car ride would save her at least half an hour, and she might get something out of Ned about his reasons for being at the conference. It occurred to her that Cal wouldn't like her to take this little jaunt, a thought that gave Rhonna pleasure, for some reason she didn't try to figure out.

Ned drove down the little winding road from Valletta toward the eastern seacoast town of Birzebugga with one hand on the wheel and the other waving somewhere between the scenery and her left thigh. Ned knew a lot about Malta, she had to admit, though his gap-toothed smile, constantly flashing her way, bothered her. He looked as if he were sure he could please any woman who even briefly took his eye and had been successful at pleasing too many of them. He was attractive enough in his way, with burly shoulders, thick thighs, thick neck and thick lips, though not her type at all.

What is my type, anyway? Rhonna wondered. Since meeting Cal Conway, a sense of what she wanted in a man had begun to coalesce like a figure of out the mists that clung in the morning to the sandy shore. She liked mystery in a man, a reason to look deeper, to find a spacious place to grow into, a jungle throbbing with living things, all bright and beautiful. She wanted a man that echoed like a giant seashell, but had roots deep in the ground like the enormous pines that surrounded her family's sprawling, weathered house, a man like her father, reliable and kind. Megan had always told her she wanted too much from a man, probably because Megan would have settled for any halfway decent guy who wanted her. Rhonna, on the other hand, would rather never marry at all than to marry someone who didn't know he was a servant of God, a steward of God's creation.

Rhonna smiled at herself for wishing Cal was God's man, when obviously he was a knowing, sharp, creature of his time, an artful, highly trained and subtle man who had probably tasted hundreds of women before his brief hours with her and would taste hundreds more after that. Rhonna refused to be a mere vague memory over a glass of champagne, someone taken casually between satin sheets in some exotic hotel. *I'm worth more than that*, she said to herself, and if Cal Conway didn't know it, she did. *If Christ loved me enough to die for me,* she reminded herself, *I matter. I won't throw myself away. I won't.*

"As I was saying, Ghar Dalam is only a cave," Ned Peavey told her, his voice louder and more insistent. He was leaning over so that she could see the sweat forming above his upper lip. "I think you were planning to go somewhere else. The temples are better. We could see those tomorrow afternoon. I'm going to skip the conference sessions on water pollution. What about you? Would you like to see Hagar Qim? It's down near the south end of the island. I'd like to see your face when you walk between those stones. Any one of them is taller than you are."

"What part of the conference are you really interested in, Ned?" Rhonna smiled sweetly at him, opening the car door on her side before he could rush around and do it himself. "I can't see you bothering with much of it. Who cares what international agreements are made about clear-cutting virgin forests? A man like you can cut down what he wants. Who's to stop you?" She knew she was laying it on thick, but figured Ned Peavey breathed flattery the way the rest of humanity breathed air, taking it for granted.

"You betcha, honey." Ned helped her out of the car, tucking her arm firmly under his as if she was a possession, like an umbrella or a newspaper. "Even if the conferees decide to go back to their countries and push for a world ban on private use of government land, which I mean not to happen, I'd just buy another senator and get mine. I'm used to getting mine, understand."

He looked down at her through half-closed eyes and she thought wryly to herself, as she disentangled her arm from his, that this look had gotten him the sort of women he wanted and that he knew its power. What he didn't know was that the game of looking like a pirate in a grade-D movie invited games on the part of whatever woman he was pursuing. A pirate was just what Ned Peavey looked like, Rhonna thought, a pirate deciding between a roast duck and a hunk of venison, whenever he leered down at her. It was enough to make any sensible woman either throw up or giggle.

Hiding a smile, which she pretended was a yawn, Rhonna walked fast ahead of him, eager to enter the place which the first Maltese had made their home. As she walked deep into the narrowing, lamp-lit cave, a draft of fresh, cool air dried the sweat that beaded her arms after a few moments in the Maltese sunshine. The earliest inhabitants had preferred to live in caves like the ones their ancestors had left in the ice-covered north of Europe. Even in those days, seven thousand years ago, Malta must have felt the first, desert-making African winds that were blowing across its once-green fields. For a moment Rhonna imagined herself a woman of those times, with her man at her side, trying to determine their future, to sort out their options, all of them risky. In her mind's eye, the man looked like Cal, and she wondered if he would have been less problematic in a simpler time. *Now,* she thought, *there are too many risks, too many options.* A man like Cal was free to live any way he wanted, and what he wanted seemed to be life on his own terms. He was obviously getting it.

Rhonna ignored Ned's easy, trivial chatter, as he tried to interest her in the sensual shapes of the rocks around them, worn by the continual stream of water that still trickled through the gulley that split the cave floor. Instead of listening to him, she looked at the bones of ancient animals and humans on the floor of the cave, that reached back as far as she could see, lit by tiny lanterns. The drip, drip of water made her think of how much time had passed since dwarf elephants had come to this cave to die, and early humans had gnawed on the bones of long extinct animals.

Her own hopes and fears seemed suddenly small, and for a moment, she understood how Cal probably felt--since life was short, enjoy it and don't get hooked into some dream of permanence. *Still,* she thought, *it's permanence I want, an eternity starting now and growing into God's own timeless glory, alongside a man God chooses for me. To be rooted in one piece of land, with one man, one family, not wasting my brief years using up other people like kleenex and throwing them aside for the next adventure. Cal's way isn't mine,* Rhonna said resolutely to herself, *and I'd better remember that. He's no more the man for me than Ned Peavey is. Just a lot more tempting, that's all.*

Ned suddenly put his coat over her bare shoulders, and she realized she was shivering. Her light cotton dress was no protection against the cool damp air of the cave.

"This is no place for a girl like you," he said. "You belong out in the sun. How'd you like to go back to Valletta and have lunch looking out over the harbor?" "Until two, I could," Rhonna said, wishing she could stay longer in this place where time stood still. "I'll have to leave at two. I mean to get to every session of this conference."

If Cal was here, the thought suddenly occurred to her, *he would not rush her away*. He would probably go deeper into the cave, until she could not see him beyond where the flickering lanterns stopped. He would call to her and show her where the river began, the source of water that sprang from inside the rocks. Rhonna shook her head, trying to dispel the image of Cal Conway guiding her into a darkness where he was surefooted and she might stumble. Ned Peavey's luncheon overlooking Valletta harbor was a lot safer, but did not stir her heart as did the thought of Cal taking her hand as she entered a darkness deeper than night.

"How about that," Ned said, steering her out into the light. "Never figured a girl with a sweet mouth like yours caring a hoot about what's under the national forests."

Rhonna gave him a sharp look as they got in the car. "We never said anything about what's under the national forests. Are you digging for gold or something?" She was being deliberately naive, hoping not to alarm him into caution.

"No, honey, uranium," he laughed, as if making a joke. "Uranium underneath and beautiful red marijuana-type poppies on top.

Just like your lips. There's a pretty scene I'd like to show you when you come to see me in the Adirondacks. You'll come, yes?" He leaned over the door and put his heavy face too close to hers.

"I try to live in the moment," she murmured, turning her face away and putting on her dark glasses, because her eyes hurt from the sun. "Not to make plans. Who knows if you'd want me to come and see you once this week is over? Who knows if we'll want to see each other after lunch?"

Ned seemed to realize he was pushing too hard, and spent the rest of the trip back to Valletta talking about the people who had built the low stone walls that edged the rocky fields. She wanted to get more out of him about his plans for the use of government land in the Adirondack reserve, but if he had any such plans, he wasn't telling.

When they got back to the hotel lobby, Cal was pacing back and forth across the flowered carpet and gave both of them a savage look from under his dark brows when they walked through the carved oak doors. He was wearing slim-cut white pants and a striped blue and white shirt. Its sleeves were turned back to his elbows and Rhonna found herself staring at the thick dark hair on forearms that swelled as his fists closed hard. She suddenly saw him like the man he would have been if he'd lived ten thousand years ago in the Ghar Dhalaam cave, she thought, her mind jumping back to the cool darkness where she had imagined him. There might have been a chance for the two of them in times like those, when the world was new and people were what they seemed.

"Rhonna, I'd like to speak to you privately," Cal said, taking her arm under his and clamping his elbow down hard, so she couldn't get away. "You'll excuse us, Ned?"

Ned Peavey had no choice, since Cal turned his back and propelled Rhonna across the room to a bench between two huge flower pots glistening with large, fiery red blossoms. They were so large and deep, Rhonna thought, that an exploring finger might well be chewed up and swallowed if it went too far into the magenta throat of such a plant. Cal sat her down beside him so hard her body jarred against his, and she felt the heat of his biceps through his tissue thin cotton shirt. She could see curly dark hair climbing from his chest toward his throat where the shirt was unbuttoned, then willed herself to look away. If he had been less angry or she had felt more confidence, she would have run her finger down his chest, just to see how it felt. But something told her that would have been a lot more dangerous than exploring the fierce-looking plants in the pot beside her. "You're not working for Ned Peavey, I trust," he said evenly. "You are working for me. The last thing I want is for you to share my information with him."

Rhonna leaned back against the corner of the seat and folded her arms over her chest, wanting to seal him off. Besides, she had caught his glance at the firm curves that rolled under the neckline of her flowing dress, and felt less vulnerable when she was covered up. At the same time, when his eyes moved to the tanned, bare skin of her shoulders and neck, she could feel them jump-start her heart, making her tremble for a moment. She looked down so she wouldn't have to see his brown eyes staring at her, hard as the polished rocks she used to pick up when she walked along the shore.

"My time is my own, as we agreed," she said. "As long as you get your three hours a day, I'm free to do as I please. I promised I'd be back for the opening session this afternoon, and I'm here. You remind me of those medieval kings that kept falcons on their arms for hunting, and expected them to wear hoods over their eyes when they're not at work."

Cal relaxed a little, a tight little smile widening his mouth."You do remind me a little of a falcon. The peregrine, I'd guess. The one that keeps travelling. Something about the way you hold your chin up and the way your eyes glint when you're angry. Well, what have you been hunting?"

Rhonna wanted to tell him she had been pumping Ned for information. Something in her hungered for this man's approval, but for that reason she would not allow herself to seek it. *Cal Conway might think he could wear me on his wrist and keep me tied to him and his interests, but I have to let him know I'm my own person.* Besides, she intended her own investigative reporting would go into her stories, not his. She wouldn't babble what she had learned just because she wanted Cal's eyes to warm up. Let him hunt down his own stories, instead of lolling around on the countess's yacht. But she would throw him something, just to let him know her visit with Ned hadn't been entirely recreation.

"Ned invited me to visit his Adirondack spread," she said, her long, slim fingers caressing her smooth arms, which were still crossed over her chest as if she were freezing. She wasn't. She was too warm, as she always felt when Cal was next to her. "He's got plans for some government land he's buying."

A blast of dry, hot desert air came in the window and blew a lock of hair into her eyes. Before she could reach up, Cal had smoothed it back, his fingers glancing over her face lightly.

"I'll bet he does. He no doubt has plans for you, too. Did he tell you what he's going to do with the land if he can steal it from the government?"

"He'll be growing flowers," Rhonna said innocently, not wanting to mention the uranium. Some things she would save for her own article. Cal had enough inside leads. "The kind that'll soon go up in a puff of smoke, I guess."

Cal laughed, his eyes warming as he saw her hand drop to her lap and stop protecting her body from his gaze. "You put it so well. Have you done some writing yourself, Rhonna Moran? You have a sharp mind and a tongue to go with it."

Rhonna hoped he wasn't seeing the blood rise to her cheeks. No matter how tan she got, her blushes showed through. They had been the curse of her teenage life and kept her from making any close friends with boys. Whenever they would stare at her, or try to touch her, she would turn red and run, before they could see how much power they had over her peace of mind. For some reason, she had always seemed to attract the toughest and most confident boys, the ones whose minds were mainly on themselves, the ones who were too dangerous to mess with. For that reason, and because she had found the teenage scene too superficial and phony, she had stayed a lot to herself. In her early teens, she had discovered a youth group at the community church. The young people had been busy helping seniors maintain their homes and taking care of kids whose parents worked. They had no leisure for hanging out and getting into trouble.

"Sharp enough to keep quiet when it's not in my interest to talk," Rhonna said. "Yes, I'm working for you, and I won't talk about anything you tell me. But I'm under no obligation to tell you everything I know." She got up and started walking. "I'm having high tea with Ned Peavey, but I'll be back for the water pollution conference. Promise."

Cal raised one dark, heavy eyebrow quizzically. "I hope you like booze and hot air for lunch, since that's what you're going to get, guaranteed."

Rhonna smiled her widest, most innocent smile, feeling the dimples deepen in her cheeks. "I'd probably have gotten the same thing if I'd had lunch with you." she said. "I'll bring you home a doggie bag full of salmon mousse, okay?"

Cal's smile vanished, and his face darkened. He was still sitting on the bench, his long legs extended, arms crossed over his chest, when she left with Ned. Rhonna assumed he was brooding over how to restore the dead zones on the Oregon coastline, since she couldn't imagine him caring that much about how she spent her lunch hour. She hoped Cal hadn't seen her glance back at him.

The warm wind swept over her as she sat at the table on the hotel terrace, looking past Ned's beefy shoulder at the aquamarine water of the harbor. Though the beach was littered with trash, which seemed to drop from the nerveless, overheated fingers of natives and tourists alike, the water was clean and pure. She longed to dive into it. After hearing people argue all afternoon that other people were responsible for toxic effects of farmed fisheries, she planned to take an hour for herself in order to lie in the warm, clear water and look at the cloudless sky as it turned pink in the sunset. "I was asking you," Ned Peavey was saying, "how you got that fantastic tan. No working girl has a tan like that."

"I got it weeding potatoes," Rhonna said, smiling vaguely at him, wishing she could think of a way to make him say something more about what he planned to do with his Adirondack forest land, bought or stolen from the government. "If you went out and worked on your flower crop, like I work on my dad's potatoes, you'd get tan too. Field work's the best tanning salon there is. But I guess you hire a lot of workers to handle your land."

Ned stretched his thick arms and yawned lazily. "I don't do anything I don't have to do. That leaves me free to cultivate life. And invite my friends to cultivate it with me. And over there's a friend I haven't seen for a while, because she's been in the company of your boss, Cal Conway. I take it he *is* your boss?"

"We don't exactly have a contract," Rhonna said, only half paying attention to him. She turned her head to see who the woman was that Ned was talking about. Over by the balcony railing, she saw a tall, voluptuous woman, with thick curly black hair falling over her shoulders. She was wearing a fitted, white crinkled silk dress with a neckline that plunged from a mandarin collar to a gold belt, baring at least a square foot of darkly tanned skin. The woman sat down, lit a cigarette, kicked her elegant Gucci sandals off her feet, and smiled at Ned Peavey. She was the toothy Italian countess Rhonna had seen pictured in *People Magazine* with Cal Conway, only a few months ago, as they photo-opped their way into the Blue Grotto of Naples. Cristina Montani, her name was. Rhonna would have a hard time forgetting those hard, dark eyes, that full body, and a mouth that looked a lot more lush than was necessary for merely talking and eating.

"Thanks for the lunch, Ned," Rhonna said. "You can interface with the barefoot contessa. I've got work to do."

Cal was pacing in the lobby, looking at his watch when she came in the door, her face flushed and her hair flying every which way from what was left of the prim chignon she'd started with. She put her hands up to smooth back her hair, wishing she didn't care so much what this man might think about the way she looked. He might even think he and Ned Peavey had been up to more than a discreet, public lunch on the hotel balcony.

"It's two minutes till conference time," Cal said coldly. "I'd like to brief you on what's happening. Too bad your social schedule doesn't give us time for that."

"You can brief me while we're on the way. What do I need to know?" Rhonna walked parallel to him, but as far away as she could without running into the corridor wall. If she had thought he might prove even a little jealous of Ned, she could think again.

Call's voice was crisp and objective, as if his mind occupied a private room that she was not allowed to enter. He was giving her only what she needed to know, but nothing that would offer her an angle for a story of her own. She had been naive, Rhonna realized, to think that this man would let fall any information that could scoop his story.

"So," he finished, "you can concentrate on typing only the material that bears on getting international funding to buy forests before the private interests do. I'll get the rest myself."

"What about minerals under those forests?" Rhonna did not look at him, but walked fast, trying to keep up. She needed to take two steps to his one, and was glad she had done enough running on Southampton beaches to keep her from huffing and puffing now.

Without turning her head, she saw Cal send a sharp glance her way. "You're looking out for Ned Peavey's interests?" he said, not really asking a question. Apparently he'd already made up his mind to distrust her. "And you said you weren't easy."

"You think salad niçoise is enough to buy my soul?" Rhonna tried to keep her tone light, but the next words slipped out with sharp, ugly edges. Until she said them, she hadn't realized how jealous she was of women Cal Conway had been with.

"Besides, Ned was rolling his eyes at Cristina Montani as much as he rolled them at me. I guess you know she's here." Rhonna took a deep breath and let it out slowly.

Maybe she could blow the cool of this unflappable man, letting him know she had his number down to the last digit. *If he thinks I can be fooled into bed by some sentimental slop he's dumped on dozens of women before me, he can forget it.* She was no potato with zits, no dumb country girl who could be dominated and won by a man who courted a countess one minute and in the next, expected a farmer's daughter to unlock the door between their bedrooms.

"Cristina shows up wherever Ned is." Cal didn't miss a step as he spoke. "She's got some kind of sonar built into her that goes blip whenever that guy changes course. Probably had it surgically implanted in place of a heart."

If Rhonna had hoped to open a crack in Cal's close-kept private life, she was disappointed. Cal could be expected to say something uncomplimentary about Cristina, just to keep Rhonna on his hook. Had Rhonna felt more confident, she would have snapped back that Cal could have checked Cristina's body for scars during the romantic interlude at the Blue Grotto, but she was not confident at all. Probably Cal had his reasons for covering up his relationship with Cristina. Rhonna couldn't help wishing those reasons included wanting to impress her with his cynicism, but she was pretty sure Cal's main reason for keeping his Cristina-connection off the agenda was his desire to protect his sources.

If there was anything she had come to know about him in their brief association, it was his intense concentration on getting the story he wanted. *Getting me into bed is only a side issue,* Rhonna thought, *a dessert he could enjoy or do without, as circumstances allow.* He was too interested in the conference and what journalistic good it could do him to veer toward the personal for any reason. Probably even Cristina, despite their presumably passionate interlude in the Blue Grotto, was no more important to him than his temporary secretary was. For some reason she couldn't fathom, this thought was comforting to Rhonna, and she began to feel calmer, less hostile toward Cal, as they settled down side by side in the press section of the conference room.

As the first sessions progressed, Rhonna found she was able to type both her own notes and Cal's on a split screen. She hoped she could find a way to siphon off her story from his computer. Perhaps she could find an excuse to take the computer into her hotel room and move her material safely into her own laptop. Luckily Cal didn't look at what she was typing, but kept his eyes on the speakers and their charts at the center of the stage. The thought came over her that he trusted her, and Rhonna blushed, feeling guilty at her intent to gather her own material on his time.

She was not stealing anything from him, Rhonna reassured herself, since her reflections on what she was hearing were her own. As she typed out the words of speakers from around the world explaining the loss of oxygen that earth would suffer from the wholesale slaughter of trees, Rhonna felt her heart grow cold and frightened. The situation was worse than she had thought. If the cutting was not checked, the world would be without trees in fifty years. Trees would be history, and human beings would have to live under glass domes with artifical oxygen pumped in. The population of countries that had no money for such technology would simply die. Her grandchildren, if the world wasn't too toxic for her to have any, would never walk in the shadow of giant pines or see the sunlight sift down through the waving branches and dapple the ground.

Before she realized that a tear was running down her face, Rhonna felt Cal's finger wiping it away. She felt like a fool, but was glad he didn't smile as he touched her cheeks. Rhonna had had no idea the situation was so bad, so hopeless. All the governments of the world seemed to want was the money rich men gave them so that the forests could be ripped off the earth. *Next will be the minerals underneath,* she thought, remembering Ned Peavey. Men like him were grave-robbers, taking the bones of the earth once the flesh was gone. They were devils, picking over the remains of an earth consecrated by the Creator. *Lord, deliver us from the Ned Peaveys of this world,* Rhonna prayed. *Let us be stewards of your earth, not pillagers.*

"It's over for now," Cal said in her ear. "I think you've had about enough, anyway. Let's get some dinner."

"No, thanks," Rhonna answered, against the will of her heart, which was doing a dance inside her, wanting what her head didn't want. The thought of a dinner with Cal on the balcony, their faces nearly touching over the little candlelit table, made her want to say yes, yes, nothing but yes. But she had to get her stuff out of the computer and onto her flash drive before Cal found it, or there was no hope of her own story. No story, no tax money for the farm. Rhonna found herself reducing every act to that stark reality, and wished she could explain to Cal why she had to. *Somehow,* she thought, *he might understand, caring about nature as he does. But I can't risk it now.*

"I'd like to go over these notes for errors, while everything's still fresh in my mind," was all she said, keeping her tone cool, so he wouldn't push the offer.

Cal seemed not to be the sort who needed to push, Rhonna had noticed before. If she wanted to be alone, so be it. He obviously had other fish to fry. Absurdly, though she had no intention of saying yes, she wanted him to push her just a little. She would not have been able to refuse, if he had let her know he really wanted her company, enough to open up and say so. But Cal left her at her door and paused only a moment before striding off down the hall, not stopping at his own room.

Rhonna wondered if he was going to hunt down Cristina Montani, and tried not to think about the leisurely dinner the two were probably going to have in the sunset while she was disentangling her notes from Cal's computer. It wasn't easy to split-screen her notes and transfer them to her flash drive. She stayed up late going over their materi- al, while the warm, damp night air blew in through her window. At midnight, she finally went to bed, hoping to hear Cal's door open and close. She lay awake for several hours, but she didn't hear any sound from his room. As she fell asleep, she felt tears on her cheeks, but this time Cal's fingers were not there to wipe them away.

Chapter Three

Rhonna woke up with sunshine streaming through the window and perspiration forming like a film all over her body. She sat up fast, thinking this heat meant it must already be noon, but the clock by her bed said only seven. An hour to swim, Rhonna said to herself, remembering the clear turquoise water she had seen from the hotel balcony. She pulled on her electric blue maillot bathing suit, which she had packed as an afterthought, knowing it would not take up any valuable space. The suit was made of a tissue silk, so delicate that she could wad it up in the fist of one hand. Even though the legs were not cut fashionably high, she feared the local men would find it too brazen. Well, she would be spending her time in the water, not lolling on the rocky little beach, so few people would see her.

Rhonna pulled her white jeans on over her suit and wrapped a large, luxurious hotel towel around her shoulders. *The chignon will never make it through a strenuous swim,* she thought. Better tuck the whole mess into a thick braid, which she could pin neatly to the back of her head. She slipped into her thongs and padded down the hotel corridor, pausing in spite of herself in front of Cal's door. No sound in there. He was either asleep or enjoying himself somewhere else. Rhonna shrugged and left the hotel, finding her way down to the beach. *He had a right, after all,* Rhonna acknowledged, *to spend the night wherever he wanted and with anyone who struck his fancy.* She had an irrational hope that the lucky woman wasn't Cristina Montani, but tried not to think about the handsome, dark contessa. Rhonna was out of Cristina's league and evidently out of Cal's too. Those two moved in their own world, lived by different rules, breathed different air. If the atmosphere ever got so full of carbon dioxide that the human race had to live under expensive domes, people like Cal and Cristina could afford one of their own. She herself and her kind, the ordinary people, would wind up crowded together or dead. *Unless,* Rhonna thought, pulling off her jeans at the edge of the sparkling water and tossing her towel on the sand beside them, *the trashing of the earth can be stopped. Cal and I are on the same side of that issue, anyway. God is too,* Rhonna was sure. At least she and Cal shared that much of a faith in creation's goodness. It had been good when God made it, even though man had done his best to avoid taking care of what he had been given. *Dominion over nature is what man has always wanted,* she thought, *while God offers us stewardship. We were too greedy, and now we'll pay the price. Here we were given the garden of Eden, and we had to steal what was forbidden. How many times do we have to fall from paradise before we get it that the earth is the Lord's? How many hurricanes and heat waves have to happen before we get it that our love of luxury and ease has made the climate crazy?*

Thinking of herself and Cal as part of a team to keep the earth's trees from becoming history, Rhonna smiled with a sudden, joyful burst of energy and plunged into the water. It was warm, and caressed her body softly, not like the brisk attack of the cold Atlantic surf she was used to. Rhonna didn't have to swim hard in order to warm up, as she did with an ocean plunge. She swam far out toward the yachts that were moored well offshore, trusting in her strength as a swimmer and a lifetime of experience in pounding waves. She had no fear of this gentle, lapping water.

After she got near the boats, Rhonna flipped over on her back and floated, letting the sun warm her face and the water cradle her. For a moment she found herself imagining that Cal was beside her, their fingers touching across the water, their bodies gliding side by side. Then she pushed the thought away, not wanting to remember that he had probably spent the night with Cristina.

Her ears were underwater, so she didn't hear the roar of an approaching speedboat. It wasn't until she felt the throbbing vibration of the boat shaking her that Rhonna's body tightened. She had a momentary spasm of terror that the propeller would drive its blades into her flesh, before she started to dive.

Suddenly strong arms seized her and pulled her deeper underwater than she could have taken herself. She held her breath until she felt like she was going to burst. When the arms pulled her back up to the surface, she opened her eyes, took an enormous breath, coughed, and saw that it was Cal Conway holding her. He shook the water off his face and hair, then shook her.

"Looks like you had in mind to swim all the way to Italy," he said roughly, as if he would have been glad if she had tried and not made it.

Then he yelled at the driver of the speedboat, which had just spun around and was coming back toward them. "Watch it, Cristina. You want to add manslaughter to your list of sins?"

The contessa's voice was low and warm as she laughed back at him. "Sorry, darling. I saw no one. Who could dream of an accident on such a heavenly morning? See you back at the yacht, no?"

The boat veered and carried Cristina, black curls flying, toward a luxurious, white vessel with green trim and a tricolor flag. *So,* Rhonna thought, *that was where Cal Conway had spent the night.* Not exactly thrashing through his notes, as he had claimed he spent most nights on assignment. She felt her heart hardening like a rock, thinking that its weight would sink her. If she had hoped a common purpose meant God had sent Cal to her, she could forget about it. *If he's Cristina's man,* she said to herself, *he could never be mine.*

Cal treaded water, his face a few inches away. He smoothed his unruly hair back, tightening the skin on his face for a moment so that he had an almost oriental look. A thick mat of hair lay flat on his chest, dark and shining.

"You might have brought Ned Peavey along to take care of you," he said, his voice even and cold. "He'd have been willing enough."

"I don't need a keeper," Rhonna said, her eyes suddenly blinded with tears. "I've always taken care of myself. Always will, thanks."

She flipped down deep and swam a few minutes underwater, hoping he would lose track of her. If being on the yacht with Cristina was where he wanted to be, she would make it easy for him. He could go back and have a champagne and caviar breakfast, with Cristina as a side dish. That was just fine with Rhonna. She finally re-surfaced only to find that Cal was swimming slightly ahead of her, his long, strong legs, with calf and thigh muscles knotted, kicking at a leisurely rate. He turned his head slightly.

"I'll see you home, if you don't mind," Cal said. "I can't afford to lose another secretary. Mumps is bad enough. Suicide is out of the question."

Rhonna thought of Cristina waiting for Cal's return, and smiled, turning her head away from him.

"Almost as bad as losing a rainforest tree," she called back. "Or a story. Such a big heart you have."

She struck out at a diagonal, wanting to put him behind her. It was humiliating to have him swimming ahead of her no matter how hard she stroked.

Cal didn't reply, but changed course, putting himself maddeningly in her way. He was going to run interference for her whether or not she wanted him to. What did he think, there were killer sharks in the harbor? That she would faint, belly up, and need saving? Rhonna took a deep breath, put her head down and did her hardest, fastest crawl toward shore. But when she got there, Cal was already waiting for her, bare wet legs apart, hands on narrow hips, the thick hair on his chest and legs already drying in the hot sun.

"Come on," he said. "We have about twenty minutes for breakfast and a rundown on today's conference. "Race you to the hotel." This time, his tone was neutral, and she could even detect a little warmth. He seemed to have forgotten about Ned Peavey.

Maybe Ned and Cristina sort of cancel each other out, Rhonna figured. Today, both she and Cal would start even, with no grudges held. Rhonna grabbed her jeans and towel, then ran a close second to Cal all the way back to the hotel, trying not to notice the stares of the Maltese men, who apparently never before in their lives had seen a pair of female legs.

All during the Friday morning conference, she sat beside Cal, trying not to look at him, though she knew when he turned slightly to look at her. He didn't look at what she was typing, Rhonna was thankful to observe, honoring her request not to. She said it bothered her to have someone watch her as she typed. That was true, if not all the truth, and he accepted that. It wasn't too hard for him to forget about the computer, she guessed, as he was totally absorbed in what was being said by the representatives of the tropical countries, whose turn it was to speak. They objected to the efforts of industrialized countries to tell them they couldn't use their resources to gain a decent standard of living for their people.

"Maybe the U.S. and Europe should offer to help them build solar panels or something. Then they wouldn't have to chop down their trees." she whispered to Cal, who nodded and made an approving okay sign with thumb and forefinger.

During a break he turned his back on Ned Peavey, who was staring at them, and said, "Tell your admirer that idea of yours. Maybe he'll decide to diversify his investments."

Rhonna wasn't sure if he was talking about Ned's uranium or his cocaine poppies. For the first time she felt a stab of sorrow that she couldn't talk freely to Cal, couldn't share their information. But if she trusted him with what little she knew, and he ran with it, there went her story. *Every time I race against Cal, I lose,* Rhonna told herself. She wouldn't take the risk of telling him the little she knew about Ned Peavey.

"I liked the notes you took yesterday," Cal said, shortening his long stride to match hers as they walked down the hall at the end of the morning's conference. "You got just about all the names of government stooges. The ones who the big companies bribe to get forest land."

"I missed some of the Brazilians, though." Rhonna felt easy, as if she was talking to herself. Sometimes Cal felt like that—another self, someone she knew like a twin with the same memories. "Couldn't spell the names."

"You got enough for me to figure out exactly who they were." Cal smiled down at her when they got to her door. "Bad spelling is the infirmity of noble minds, they say."

"Well, as long as you know I spell badly only in Portuguese." Rhonna, leaning back, her fingers tight on the door handle.

Cal put one arm up against the door, easily, naturally, as if he felt no excitement at how close their bodies were.

"The conference stops early for the weekend," he said. "I'm planning to go south to Qrendi for a couple of days to see the temples down there. I'd like to see them with you."

The slight smile faded fast from his face and she saw the little twitch in his tight jaw that she had noticed that first day at the airport. It suddenly struck her that he might be feeling just as resistant to unfamiliar sensations as she was. His body seemed poised to run the other way, and she wondered if he wanted her to say yes or no.

"Qrendi's only a half hour bus ride from here," she said, frowning a little, not sure how she could avoid what "weekend" usually meant in a man's vocabulary. "I could meet you for the day."

"You'd have your own hotel room on the beach, Rhonna," he said, flipping out a key and opening her door. "Nobody's going to jump your bones in a sacred shrine." He held the door open for her and smiled, a tight, wary smile that made her wonder if he hadn't just such a plan in mind.

"On the beach?" Rhonna wished she had brought along her snorkelling gear. She knew that the waters of Malta's south shore were clear enough that she could see grains of sand through them. And maybe Cal had nothing more in mind than a sightseeing tour. *A night with Cristina on her yacht may have sated him for the moment,* Rhonna thought. Why should she suppose that she could compete with this Italian contessa, whose languorous, possessive eyes seemed to eat up whatever they saw? Why should Cal feel there was any competition anyway? *In any case, I can take care of myself, with the grace of God, as long as Cal spends the night behind a wall.*

"If I get my own room, I'll go, thanks."

"Let's try for some sleep first," he said, and she thought he lingered for a moment before closing her door behind him. "See you at one."

It was only when she was inside the room and alone that Rhonna considered the fact that he had a key to her door. She took off her damp suit and lay down on the bed, feeling the hot, wet air drift over her. In the next room, Cal's bed creaked and she imagined lying down next to him, drifting off to sleep in his arms, his lips on hers. Resolutely, she put all images aside, turned on the fan, and pulled the sheet over her. In her dreams, Cal Conway lay so close to her that their two drenched, overheated bodies were twined into one and she could feel his breath on her mouth, his hands searching her skin. She pushed the image out of her mind and inwardly repeated her favorite prayer, *Not my will but yours, Lord, be done in my life.* She could almost feel the touch of Christ like a kiss on her forehead, and her anxiety went away.

All the way to Qrendi, Cal kept his eyes on the road, his jaw clenched shut as if he planned to say nothing and spoke only against his better judgment. She wondered if he had waked from the same kind of dreams that had troubled her.

"You've read the guide book," he finally said. "What do you know about Hagar Qim? Or is that the sort of information you share only with Ned Peavey?"

He pronounced the name of the temple with offhanded correctness, "Edger-eem." She wouldn't have known how it was said, and was glad he had given her a clue. If he hadn't told her, she would have said it wrong and felt like a fool. Again, Rhonna was uncomfortably aware of her ignorance and of Cal Conway's easy grace in new situations and places.

It was as if he had been everywhere before, even here, and pretended not to remember, maybe in order to bring her out, make her talk. Knowing how much she had to hide from him, Rhonna decided to talk only about the temple. *It would be too easy to let him con me into telling all I know or at least suspect about Ned Peavey's game-playing at the conference.* As he parked the car, Rhonna's eyes met Cal's, locked for a moment, and then she turned away, toward the imposing granite outline of the temple. Ned's wide shadow was between them even on neutral territory, and maybe Cal knew that as well as she did.

As they walked through the gate in the temple's massive stone wall, Rhonna felt Cal's hand brush hers. He had to bend a little to clear the stone lintel that lay across the two side pillars. Apparently the ancient Maltese had not been much taller than their contemporary replacements.

"Why didn't the old inhabitants make statues of men, do you think?" His tone was respectful, for a change, not patronizing, and Rhonna felt a bit more self-confident than usual.

"The men had their place, but the temple belonged to the mother. That's her statue, over there, without a head." She gestured at the obese, fertile form of the immense, headless stone goddess. "Archeologists used to call these female forms Venuses, but now they think the statues were made to honor motherhood. We could learn something from the people who used to be here."

The sun was blazing hot, and she wiped her damp forehead with her forearm.

Cal took off his floppy straw hat and put it on her head. "You'll fry that lovely skin of yours, if you aren't careful," he said. "Five freckles already, and counting."

He took her by the hand and pulled her into a shady little stone room. The roof was gone, but the thick, tall stone walls kept the area sunless and cool.

"Maybe the mother goddess has no head because in those days men didn't consider a woman's head important," Cal said.

His brown eyes glinted, and she wondered if he was teasing her again. If so, she wouldn't take the bait.

"I think the reason all the goddesses' heads are gone," she said levelly, trying not to notice how close to her he was standing, "is that when the land dried up and the people had to leave, the heads were all they could take with them. No one could carry those two ton statues in the kind of boats they had then."

"Good idea," Cal nodded. "One of these days maybe you'll write a book of your own about this place. I've seen the way you put words together. Your notes read like finished copy." Rhonna felt herself blushing and turned away from him.

"So women's heads are important, after all?" She put her hands behind her nervously and stepped back a little.

"To me, yes. I can't speak for other men." Cal slipped the hat off her head with both hands, then let them slide down behind her, imprisoning her in the circle of his arms. The slight smile turned grim and preoccupied as he let the hat fall and held her two arms behind her easily with one hand. He hooked the other around her neck, forcing her face upwards so that her lips landed hard on his.

Rhonna tried to pull her hands out from behind her, but he had them in a grip like handcuffs. She felt her shoulders grind against the stone wall, while the whole length of him seemed to melt into the front of her, turning her skin hot. Her insides felt molten enough to overflow, and her hands went limp behind her. He released them, then ran his fingers over her back with increasing pressure, as if he were planning to take her apart and explore her from within.

Why don't I push him away, Rhonna asked herself furiously, feeling her arm move around him, feeling his hard, knotted muscles slide under her fingers. He must think she would be easy, that he could have her anytime he wanted. *And the awful thing is that he could*, Rhonna thought, *because my brains are turning into cornmeal mush along with the rest of me.* Her body felt like it wanted nothing but to open itself to Cal's insistent urging, as if he had a right to her and could easily take what belonged to him.

His hand wound into her chignon, and when he moved it fast, her hair came tumbling down around her shoulders. "I like it this way," he said, his voice thick and slow. "You should never tie it up. It should be free. You should be free." He ran the fingers of both hands through her hair, starting at the neck, caressing it, then lifting the heavy waves so that they played around his fingers.

The word 'free' struck Rhonna like a blow. Free was what she had always wanted to be, not a servant to some man's whims and notions, not feeling she had to please, to be more, in order to be loved. *God's like that,* Rhonna suddenly thought, *and so is Dad, loving me for who I am.* It would be a long time, if ever, before she found a man like him, a man who knew how to love without turning the loved one into himself, turning her to his own purposes. If there was anything Rhonna feared and hated, it was being used, and if there was any man who could use her, it was this one. She pushed his hands aside, running out of the roofless room into the blasting sun. Her heart was pounding all over her chest, and her legs shook so they could hardly carry her. *Another moment, and I would have done anything he asked,* Rhonna thought. *Only he wouldn't have asked. He would have just taken. That's Cal's way. Never mind what was best for me.*

The tears stung her eyes as she thought how he would have forgotten her as he had all the rest. Probably he would tell Cristina Montani of his little adventure in the temple and the two of them would have laughed at her over their Dom Perignon champagne. The trouble was, after that kiss, how was she going to put him out of her mind, sit beside him as they worked, trying not to imagine his hands all over her, his mouth against hers, breathing into her until she came alive with wanting him. After that kind of kiss, there was no way back. He would take her further and further until she lay helpless and longing in his arms. *No,* she said to herself, *I made a promise to God and to my own soul that love has to come first, before this crazy desire knocks me flat. So this is temptation. No wonder we need grace to fight back, if this tidal wave of wanting is what the enemy is like.*

With a sob she couldn't swallow, Rhonna took off down the long causeway toward the shore cliffs, where the small companion temple to the larger one rose against the blazing blue sky. When she got inside, she waited, feeling like her heart was going to bang its way up through her throat. But Cal apparently hadn't followed her. He was not a man to put out energy in pursuit of what he could get with a finger snap from someone else.

For a moment Rhonna was sorry he had not cared enough to come after her. Then she reminded herself that the more distance she could place between her and Cal when they were alone, the safer she would be. *Only a few more days*, she told herself, *and we'll be on the plane home.* Probably they would never meet again after landing at Kennedy. *If I can just hold him at arm's length until we say goodby,* Rhonna thought, *I'll feel like I belong to God and myself again.* Cal wouldn't be able to laugh with Cristina, or whoever his next woman would be, at Rhonna's easy tumble into his bed.

She stood in the middle of the temple, before a mushroom-shaped pedestal. Her arms stretched out in front of her, palms turned up. In those ancient days worshipers here had not known God, only grasped at a shadow of divinity. Now she could call down His grace on the place they had wanted to consecrate but had not known how. Spontaneously, she began to move in a slow dance, her face turned up to the sun, her hips swinging in slow circles. It was a kind of prayer-dance that she used to do at home on the beach, her heart overflowing with too much reverence to pray in mere words.

She let her neck move in circles too, so that her hair drifted across her face, then flew behind her again. As she danced, she sang a wordless song in her soft, low voice. Her arms lifted and twined together above her head, and she swayed as she had when

Cal's arms held her. It was as if, for a moment, she were not herself, but someone from long ago, dancing out her longing for love, for the touch of a particular man who would set her moving in slow circles, like a tree in the wind.

"Lovely," said Cal's slow, drawling voice. "You'd make some belly dancer."

Her eyes flew open and she saw him leaning with folded arms against the tall stone lintel, his eyes warm and his cheeks flushed.

"You had no right to watch," she said hotly, pulling down her tank top hard, so that it covered her midriff again. "That was private."

"You're right." Cal stayed at the door, at least. It seemed he wanted no repeat of the scene in the other temple. "Think of me as an accidental tourist looking for local color. I wish I had my camera to catch the resident nymph in action."

Rhonna hoped Cal wouldn't see the blush under her deepening sunburn. She wanted to take his mind off her and hers off him.

"That hole in the stone over there," she gestured, trying to keep her voice cool, "do you think it's one of those megaphone holes the priests called through to scare the crowds?"

"I've seen the same kind of holes in the temple at Delphi," Cal said, going over to inspect the one she had pointed to. He called through the hole in a big bass voice that roared through the temple.

"Rhonna Moran has the body of a goddess," he called. "No, make that an angel." He turned back to Rhonna, smiling. "Angels are presumably thinner than the local goddesses."

Rhonna walked through the temple, not looking at him. She talked to cover her confusion. "It could be that the people who built these temples left for Greece when the weather got too hot. I read that the climate changed for the worse about three thousand years ago. Maybe they tried to build their temples all over again in Greece."

Cal nodded as he fell in beside her. "I said before there's a book in you. I hope you write it."

As they came out of the temple into the sunlight and stood on the cliffs that looked toward Libya, Rhonna looked up at him quickly, taking in the set of his jaw and the stubble just forming on it.

"For that, I'd need to come back and stay a while."

Cal's stride slowed to match hers. "That could be arranged," he said. "I'd love to take you to Gozo, the island just north of here. It's like a little Paris, like Paris probably was a hundred years ago. Only you'd better not dance. The Maltese men would be all over you, and I'd have to beat them off."

His body suddenly stiffened, and he pointed below them on the rocky beach. "Look there. A boat's drifting toward the rocks. Some kids in it." He looked up and down the beach. "Nobody around. Run back to the gate and tell the guard to call for help. I'm going down."

Be careful, she wanted to call after him, but Cal was already climbing like a cat down the cliff, his hands and feet finding roots and rock to hold onto. She could see his dark red hair, gleaming in the brilliant sun, disappear over the edge, and she felt an enormous loss, as if she was never going to see him again. He had ceased to be hers and disappeared like a dream.

Rhonna had a feeling that he would always disappear, and that nothing she was or might become would change Cal's assertion of his essential separateness. *I'm like that too*, Rhonna reflected as she ran for the guard's kiosk at the entrance to the temple grounds. For that reason, she knew how deeply his independence was a part of him, and how little chance she had of changing it. As her feet pounded on the hard, parched earth, Rhonna realized that she was running in the opposite direction from Cal and that she probably would always be doing just that. She ran faster, thinking of the waves rolling in from Africa, tossing the boat and Cal as well against the rocks. *Lord,* she prayed, *help him save the children. Be with him, even if he doesn't know you.*

By the time the guard had called the shore patrol and they had taken Rhonna with them down the stony, narrow road to the beach, she could see Cal swimming out toward the little boat overturned in the surf. His long, powerful arms beat the water, subduing it into carrying him where he chose to go. Though the strong current tried to pull him out to sea, he swam at an angle, getting always closer toward the boat, and the bobbing heads of the young swimmers.

"Come back," the shore patrol captain yelled through his bullhorn. "You cannot help them in this rough water. A storm is coming. We have sent for a patrol boat."

Cal turned his head toward them for a second, so Rhonna knew he had heard. Then he put his head deep in the water and swam hard, going for the swimmer who had begun to sink, her hair dipping beneath the waves. As the girl sank out of sight, Rhonna held her breath, then breathed again when she saw Cal bob up again, one arm curved around the girl's neck. He swam with the other until he had gripped the overturned sailboat. When he had made sure she was sitting safely on the boat, Cal went for the other swimmer and brought him in to shore.

"He needs CPR," Cal said, laying the boy's limp body on the rocks. "Can anybody do it? Rhonna? Okay, get started. I'm going back for the girl."

"But no, Signore, it is too dangerous." The captain of the shore patrol caught at Cal's elbow. "The surf is building up. One of our ships will come soon to help."

"No time." Cal shook his arm loose. "That boat has about five minutes before it breaks up." He dove into the surf, which broke high in the air, then hung for a moment like wet lace.

"Such a *huomo*," the captain said admiringly. "A real man. And he is not even one of us."

"Not an Italian, surely," said another. "Only Maltese men do such things."

The Italian captain glared at him, then looked back out toward the boat with his binoculars.

Rhonna was still breathing mouth-to-mouth into the half-drowned boy's lungs when Cal pulled the girl in and started sight of Cal, bending over the prostrate girl, his mouth hard against hers. A lightning twinge of painful pleasure shot through her body. She couldn't help imagining that she herself might sometime lie under him in just such a way, her head tipped back to drink his kisses, coming to life as his breath flowed into her. *No, Rhonna, don't go there,* she warned herself.

The boy began to stir and cough. Rhonna sat him up and pounded his back. At the same time, the girl Cal was working on coughed up sea water and rolled over on her side.

"Funny thing, how when something like this happens, you can't help praying," Cal murmured to Rhonna. "Maybe some part of me still believes in God, at least in emergencies."

Rhonna smiled at him. "Then may all your life be an emergency," she said. "I think that's true of mine."

"Hold it, Miss," called a voice. "You're on camera. Tony, you get a shot of the blonde, and I'll get the guy. Mister, you look like you dislocated your shoulder out there when you hit that rock."

Rhonna felt embarrassed and got up fast. It was Cal's rescue effort, not hers, and she wanted him to get the credit on the Maltese evening news, if that was what these video cameramen were representing. Cal was holding his elbow with one hand, and she could see the gash in his left bicep where he had hit a sharp rock. A twinge shook her, as if it had been she, not he, who had been cut.

"He pulled them out," she said, gesturing at Cal. "Better talk to him." She pulled a white cotton kerchief out of her shoulder bag. "Cal, could you use a sling?"

"Yes, thanks. A tourniquet's more like it." He glanced at his watch, then, with one practiced hand, twisted the kerchief around his upper arm to stop the bleeding. As they approached the gate, he asked Rhonna, "Where'd you learn to do CPR like that? I thought only paramedics knew to put their hands where you did." "I grew up on the South Fork," Rhonna waved goodby to the guard, not letting him kiss her hand as he tried to. "Did at least ten CPR rescues a year. We all learned to do it when we were kids."

She stopped to inspect his wound before they got into the car. "Hey, you might need stitches for that. It's deep, and it's still bleeding."

"Not the way it was." Cal checked his watch again and loosened the tourniquet. Then he held the reddening cloth over the wound. "I owe you a new scarf. Let me take you over to the boutique at the hotel after dinner. I'd like to get you a blue silk one, to match your eyes. One big enough to make a sarong. You've got a body made for sarongs."

"Unless a story comes up for both of us in Tahiti, I guess you'll never know," Rhonna said sharply, covering a surge of warm gladness at his approval. She tried to imagine the sort of story they might cover on a South Sea Island. "Wells poisoned by a jet airport, maybe. Or whatever passes for environmental news on Tahiti."

"Cocaine plantation discovered among the hibiscus blossoms." Cal broke off a red flower from a bush near the car and tucked it behind her ear. "You have in mind, maybe, to check out Ned Peavey's plantation in Tahiti?"

Rhonna started to say that she was heading for Peavey's poppies in the Adirondacks, but thought better of it. Her quickness to spill all she knew to this man made her nervous. It would be easier if she saw less of him, but that would mean no more banter back and forth, no more walks where her hand brushed his, and no more of those sudden kisses that shook her to the soul. Rhonna bit her lip and looked down.

Before he opened the car door for her, Cal lifted her chin and stared into her eyes, his dark brows meeting as he frowned. "You can go where you want. I just think you should know Peavey's not to be trusted. Not around a clean type like you. When I first saw you, I..." His voice trailed off, and he turned away from her abruptly.

"You what?" Rhonna's heart pounded as if she were running hard, and she laid her hand on her throat. He would probably tell her what he had told Cristina Montani and a hundred other women. She could almost write the script, and hated being able to predict what should have been honest between them.

Whatever it was, she wanted to hear it, to believe even for a moment that the two of them had touched each other at a level so deep that it could not be forgotten or brushed off as an attempt at seduction. What she wanted was a man who would love her soul as well as her body, spirit touching spirit in a timeless act of grace. That, for Rhonna, was what marriage was about. It wasn't about romance. It was about the joining of two people in Christ. Without Him, there could be no permanence, no spiritual deepening, no love worthy of the name. That's what she wanted. Somewhere she had read that Freud once asked 'What do women want?' If he had asked her she would have told him—to be cherished in Spirit and in truth and to love back in the same way. Freud wouldn't have known what she was talking about, and probably neither would Cal.

Rhonna stood straight and looked him in the eye when he turned toward her again. "I would like to hear what you really feel," she said, aware that she was pushing him in the way her mother used to warn her would drive men off.

He seized her by both arms, so hard that they ached. "You don't want to know. It would scare you right back to your potato farm. I'm not your sort, Rhonna Moran. You'd be better off with the nice guy that took you to the senior prom."

Before she could tell him that the night of her senior prom had been spent helping her mare to foal, Cal had left her beside the open car door and gone around to the other side to start the car. What she had assumed was true. Cal was not interested in getting involved with a manure-shoveling farm girl. *My world and his are like oatmeal and caviar. They could never mix.* She had learned what she needed to know and was silent all the way back to the hotel. It was an answer to prayer, of sorts, but not the answer she wanted to hear.

Over dinner that night, Cal seemed to know she wanted to keep her distance. He didn't even try to take her red Moroccan shawl off her shoulders when they sat down, and Rhonna was just as glad. The skimpy black dress, with its spaghetti straps seemed to cover a lot less of her than it had when Megan insisted on buying it. The black jersey clung to her damp skin, and she could see the short skirt riding up her thighs under the glass table top. To his credit, Cal stared at them only once, then laid a menu in front of her.

"I'll have thighs marsala," he said, then corrected himself easily, without a blush. "Chicken marsala, that is, with hearts of palm vinaigrette. And you?"

Rhonna controlled her urge to giggle, and looked down the list for a vegetarian dish. "I like the sound of the hearts of palm thing," she said, "and the pasta provençale. Looks like that's the only dish without meat."

After ordering, he leaned forward on his elbows and looked at her face for a long time. "You're consistent, Rhonna," he said. "Something about you runs true all the way. Like the way you love animals. I can imagine you with a bumper sticker on your car, 'Be kind to animals. Don't eat them.'"

"You don't think you're consistent?" Rhonna had to smile. She did, in fact, have a bumper sticker on her battered pickup, saying just about what Cal thought it said.

"About work, yes," he said with a frown. "It's where I've put all the best in me."

"And the worst?" Rhonna wondered if he were thinking, as she was, about the affair with Cristina.

"Let's just say I put too much of my energy into things that aren't worth it." Cal said shortly pouring himself some burgundy. "And I don't like myself better for that. My mother warned me I wouldn't, sweet Christian lady that she is. She didn't raise me to be a godless egotist. I'm thinking now that she was right." His voice dropped and a sudden shadow passed over his face. "Here, have some wine." He looked as if he were making an effort to put the shadow aside. "The color of it matches your shawl. By the way, you don't need a cover-up in here. It's got to be ninety degrees."

Cal moved his chair around the little table until their arms touched, then lifted the shawl from her shoulders and laid it over the back of her chair, just brushing her skin with his fingertips. "That's an improvement."

His eyes flashed over her moist, golden-tan skin, which gleamed against the soft black jersey. "Second time today I've wished I had a camera. Strange. I'd never noticed before how many shades of gold there are." He reached up and touched a loose tendril of her shining blond hair lightly. "The candlelight, maybe."

Rhonna blushed, hoping the dim lighting would keep him from seeing the pink spreading over her cheeks. She had to change the subject before she turned as red as the wine. "When I'm on the beach at home," she said, swirling the wine in her glass and looking into it rather than drinking, "I see different colors in the sand every day. Once I took twenty pictures of some rocks at the edge of the water. Every print turned out to have a different color."

Leaning back a little so the waiter could put the dinner plate down, Cal smiled at her. "Nothing stays the same. It's one of the joys and curses of this world."

"Some things do," Rhonna insisted stubbornly, twisting her fork into her pasta. "I've always loved my land, and always will. I love my dad and God the same way."

He looked at her curiously. "You're fortunate to feel that attachment to a place. To a person. To God. Except for my mother, I've never felt anchored, and not always to her."

"That's the second time tonight you've mentioned your mother. How long has it been since you've seen her?" Rhonna spoke shyly, not looking at him. She didn't mean to pry, but it seemed he was inviting her to go deeper, since he had spoken of his mother twice in the space of a single conversation.

Cal brushed back his unruly forelock back with one hand. "Too long. Five years. I've written some letters and called once or twice. If my father doesn't answer or cut us off, she and I talk a while. I try to get along without family. And I never really was into the idea of home. What does home mean to you, Rhonna?"

She looked into his dark eyes, seeing her face reflected in their depths. "For me? I guess it's right at my core. Home has a place in my heart reserved for it, and I can go back anytime I want, in my imagination," Rhonna answered, thinking that she and Cal were not as alike as she sometimes felt they were.

"You have to put all your energy into a person or a place. It seems to me you don't learn to care much about anything, unless you give it your complete attention. Somebody said of God, 'our hearts are restless until they find themselves in you.' I believe that. If you don't pay attention to God, to the people you love, you lose them."

"That's what you give, I've noticed," Cal said, putting down the piece of meat he had been about to eat. "You pay attention to everything. To everyone. It's as if you never saw them before." He smiled and studied her, his forehead smoothing as it seldom did. "So much fascinates you."

"Right now, this pasta is what fascinates me," Rhonna said, embarrassed to hear so much talk about herself. "Since I can't eat and talk at the same time, I'm going to shut up."

Cal followed her example, though several times he looked as if he was about to say something, then changed his mind. After finishing his dessert, he pushed his plate away and watched her eat her *blancmange*. "Not many family farms are left on the South Shore," he said, with a little crease deepening between his eyebrows. "How come yours is one of them? The taxes break most farmers."

Rhonna choked and put her spoon down. She suddenly didn't have any appetite for the snowy dessert in front of her. "I wish I could tell you the taxes won't break us," she said slowly. "They might. I'm working on the problem."

"Maybe the reason for hanging out with Peavey?" he suggested, keeping his voice light and teasing.

She stood up and pulled her shawl around her tightly. "You know how to run a good interview," she said, hoping her voice wouldn't tremble. "How to find out what you want to know. And you said you aren't consistent. I'd say you are."

"Easy, Rhonna." Cal caught her napkin as it fell from her lap and tossed it on the table. "Nothing wrong in my book if a girl wants to shake down Ned Peavey for a few bucks."

"It would be wrong in mine," Rhonna said, not caring that tears were standing in her eyes. "But I guess you don't know me that well. Whenever I think maybe you do, I get smacked upside the head."

She ran through the dining room, knowing people were staring at her, knowing Cal thought she was an idiot to mind being read wrong. *The reason I mind,* she wished she could say to him, *is that more than anything, I want to be understood, to be accepted, to be loved for who I am.* Just when she felt close to that with Cal, she was brought up short by that hard, mocking streak of his. That way he had of thinking everybody was as cold and worldly as he was. And if they weren't, he'd soon bring them down to his level. *Too much fooling around with* women like Cristina Montani, Rhonna thought, has turned him cynical. I'm wasting my time if I believe he'll change.

Later in the evening, when he knocked softly at her door and called her name, Rhonna pretended to be asleep. Her pillow was damp from perspiration or tears, she wasn't sure which, and she kept turning it over, trying to get it cool and dry. It was like trying to wring out her heart and get rid of all the soft, silly notions about Cal that had been boiling in it since she met him. She had to stop thinking he could feel as intensely as she did. Every time she tried, the effort ended in disappointment.

They were alike only on the surface, she and he, no matter how his ideas made him feel like an extension of herself. His closeness was a danger to her, and made the truth turn shimmering and vague. The truth was that he was out to get what he could from her, and he assumed she was doing the same with Ned. That was the world he lived in, and no number of warm moments, skin on skin, lips opening to lips, would change that truth. Giving up on the pillow, Rhonna threw it across the room and lay flat on her stomach, trying to pray. Even her prayer seemed cold and arid, like Cal. She fell asleep, finally able to ignore the throbbing of her body, which was dancing to a different tune than her mind and refused to stop.

Chapter Four

When Cal and Rhonna returned to Valletta the next morning, a message from Ned Peavey was waiting for her. Rhonna found herself hiding it from Cal, not wanting him to imagine that what he said last night was true. Fortunately, he was sifting through his own messages and seeming to be in a different mode, one where she did not exist. She watched him read the notes and toss them aside.

The desk clerk hung over the counter and smirked. "You sure got a lot of calls from Cristina Montani," he said. "The last one, she came by here and wrote. Said she was all yours, any time. You are one lucky guy, mister."

Cal glanced sideways at Rhonna, then crumpled a handful of messages. To the clerk he said in a hard voice, "You'll keep your face out of my mail, from now on. And if she calls again, you can tell her I'll be in touch sometime," he said. "Right now, I need to sleep. No calls for the next few hours." He tossed the wad ball of messages over the counter, not staying to see if the clerk caught them.

Ned's message had asked that Rhonna go on the afternoon ferry with him to Gozo, the small, rural island to the north. He promised her a party to remember, in the best hotel Gozo's capital had to offer. Rhonna read the message twice, remembering that Cal had told her Victoria, the capital, was a little Paris. She wished she could see it with him, but her practical, farmer's daughter's side said better to see it even with Ned than not to see it at all. And she would be a boat-ride away from the driving temptation to lie down beside Cal Conway and not get up till Christmas.

"Tell Ned Peavey I'll be ready at four. In time for the last ferry over," she told the hotel clerk. Cal gave her a long look, and Rhonna felt a chill, sad lump in the pit of her stomach. *The decision's made,* she said to herself, *and can't be changed. Won't be changed.* She needed to put distance between herself and Cal now, before he took her over totally. A small, still voice in her spoke words of caution, but she overrode it, sure that Ned was a lot less dangerous to her than Cal. Because she was feeling so stiff and unfeminine, Rhonna compensated by wearing her hair loose and the dress Megan had talked her into buying. The rainbow chiffon rippled around her bare legs as she walked into the lobby, hoping, against her better judgment, to meet Cal by accident. He had said he was sleeping, and apparently he was. *First things first,* she said to herself, her jaw clenched so hard it gave a little twitch, the way his so often did.

I'm obviously last on Cal Conway's list of priorities, Rhonna told herself, *He's a man I could never please.* When she saw Ned she smiled, knowing she was exactly what he had hoped she would be. At least somebody liked her the way she was. Rhonna stepped into Ned's white taxi, her heart torn down the middle. One part of her wanted Cal, wanted the hard touch of his lips, and the other wanted Ned to tell her he would give her a story that would make her reputation as a reporter. She had to be practical. This story could put her in line for a raise, in addition to paying a lump sum that might pay off the back taxes. With the raise, she stood a chance of paying this year's taxes as they came along. Being distracted by Cal was the last thing she needed. *Maybe God's giving me the chance I've prayed for,* she thought. *If that's what He's doing, I can't let it get away.* She made an effort to smile when she saw Ned waiting for her and saw in the mirror by the staircase that she had succeeded. Only someone who knew her well would have noticed that her face was pale and that the corners of her lips didn't turn up as they usually did.

When Ned hurried across the lobby, his hands out to grasp hers, Rhonna felt a sudden urge to cry. She wished it were Cal reaching out to her, Cal smiling, Cal taking her off to the little Maltese version of the Paris he loved. She kept her teeth clenched and her breath deep and calm. This was her night to learn what she needed to learn. She could already imagine herself slapping down ten thousand in cold cash in front of the tax clerk in Southhampton City Hall, God willing.

The half-hour boat ride across the gentle, moonlit sea captivated Rhonna in spite of her dark mood. She leaned on the rail of the ferry's upper deck and threw her head back, letting the wind play with her loose, flowing hair. For a moment, she could imagine Cal behind her, his long, powerful hands touching her bare shoulders. Instead, she felt Ned's arms circle around her waist. He threw his half-smoked cigar in the water, where it sizzled and floated in circles like some obscene thing fouling the pure water of Malta's bay.

Rhonna backed away and put her filmy blue scarf around her shoulders, remembering how Cal had put it there this afternoon after they had picked it out at the boutique in Qrendi. *Why does everything remind me of Cal*, she wondered, trying to smile back at Ned. Better that he not think she was entirely cold to him. But every thought, every image that floated through her mind had Cal at the other end of it, as if she was a kite and he was holding the string that kept her from soaring free. No matter how far she sailed, he had the power to draw her back to him. He and she seemed to be caught, tangled together in a web at the center of her soul, and flutter as she might, she could not pull free of him. She sighed and paced the deck beside the railing, trying not to let Ned's arm encircle her again.

"I'd like to warn you as a friend," Ned said, apparently reading her mind. "Cal Conway is one dangerous guy. You should hear the stories Cristina tells of him. And she should know."

Rhonna snapped around, both hands behind her as she leaned against the rail. "Dangerous to who, Ned? To women? Or maybe to you? Tell me. I really want to know."

"Well," he drawled. "I see I finally got your attention. Cal Conway, my dear, is a world class seducer of women. Takes one to know one, the saying goes." He licked his lips and Rhonna instinctively backed away. "Cristina says he's got a pattern. Shows a little sensitivity. Gets on a woman's wavelength by sharing her interests. Tells her what she wants to hear about herself. She'd be a great model. Or actress. Or whatever. Got the picture?"

"And you think I'm fool enough to fall for it. Is that what you're telling me?" Rhonna felt goosebumps on her arms and wrapped the thin scarf more tightly around her. Cal had been telling her she had it in her to be a writer. Could that be just a part of his game plan? Bill Kingsley said the same thing, and old Bill wasn't out for anything from her. But Bill didn't set up adjoining hotel rooms or take her to deserted places, either. His compliments, unlike Cal's, were obviously free of charge.

"Cheer up, honey," he said, moving closer to her and bending his head, so that his black beard brushed her shoulder.

"The best is yet to come. He and Cristina Montani are planning a big society wedding this summer. They even invited me, and God knows, I'm not Cal Conway's favorite person."

Rhonna swung around facing the water, her eyes closed, feeling a sharp pain slice her stomach. It was true, then. Cal was only playing with her while he waited to marry a title, a palazzo, and a permanent niche in *People Magazine.* But why did Cal's jaw work that strange, tight way when she touched him? Why did he kiss her like she was his last hope for life? *Cal's not indifferent to me,* she thought. *I could swear he's not. But why would Ned lie?* She would have to know Ned better if she was going to find out, however dangerous he might be. Breathing deeply to calm the air trembling in her throat, Rhonna took Ned's arm and walked toward the bow of the ship, which was coming up on Gozo's harbor.

"It's kind of you to look out for me," she said, lowering her eyes as her southern mother had taught her. "I appreciate it. I really do. Tell me, how long have you known Cal Conway?"

"Since his story on my logging operation in the National Forests stopped me dead ten years ago." Ned smiled grimly and lit a cigarette with one hand, bracing the matchbox expertly against his palm as he struck the match. "He's a shrewd son of a gun. Talked the wife of my foreman into testifying in court. She sang like a finch."

"Poor Ned," Rhonna said gently, half meaning it. Whoever Cal set out to get was someone to feel sorry for. "And now he's got Cristina. And maybe whatever secrets you've told her?"

Ned stopped walking and puffed on his cigar, frowning. "Where'd you hear that?" Then he smiled, as if a storm had passed quickly. "Cristina knows better than to talk about me. We have our..."

He broke off suddenly. "Look. That's her yacht anchored down there. I'd take a good guess and say she and Cal will be going to the same party we are. You mind?"

"I can live with it," Rhonna shrugged, hoping Ned had not noticed the sudden rush of blood to her cheeks. "After all, I've got his number now, thanks to you." She smiled, took his arm, and walked down the gangplank onto the pier where Ned Peavey's car awaited them. The Maltese driver gave Rhonna the obligatory leer, and she pulled her blue scarf over her low neckline, crossing her hands over her bosom. Ned gave her an amused glance as he lowered himself into the back seat.

"You don't have to cover up, honey," he said. "You're in the company of a connoisseur. I can look without sampling. At least for a while."

Again she had that uncomfortable feeling that to a man like Ned, no woman meant more than a good dinner. Using him was not something to be sorry for, Rhonna reminded herself, since he had used so many people himself. She would have to get rid of her inhibitions against deceit if she was going to deal with such a man. *But can I sink to the level of Ned Peavey and still call myself a Christian?* Rhonna wished her dad was there to ask. He saw clearly, no matter what was at stake. *What would he say? Maybe, do the ends justify the means?* He seldom gave advice, just asked questions that she should be able to ask herself. If she was going to be a journalist and not just a sleazy reporter, she had better start asking the right questions now.

"The way you look at your Adirondack forest?" She arched one eyebrow delicately.

"I said, for a while." Ned told the driver to pull into the hotel lot. "The better the view, the less patience I have." He smiled down at her. "That goes for trees and beautiful women both."

"Yet you'd cut down three hundred foot trees to get the minerals underneath," Rhonna said, trying to keep her tone light. "I can't help wondering if you'd do the same to a woman."

"If she glowed like uranium, I guess I would," Ned said, helping Rhonna out of the car. "Some women are like that," he added, his fingers curving hard around her slender waist. "You're one of them."

Oh, give me a break, Rhonna said to herself. *Thank God, I'm not so simple as to fall for such stuff.*

As they went up the stone staircase that led into the main building, she could see the sparkling water that reflected the hotel. *It was like walking into the Emerald City,* she thought, a shock for someone like herself, right off the farm. She was determined not to let her shyness show, and lifted her chin at a militant angle.

"I like the way you do that," Ned whispered. "The way you toss your hair back and harden that pretty chin of yours. I like a fighter."

"I wonder if you really want the uranium under those trees or you just want to win a fight," Rhonna said, turning abruptly to him, forgetting that she was going to be subtle. Guile came hard to her and easily fell away.

Ned looked surprised. "Both. Don't look so shocked. I could run the whole Northeastern U.S. for the next century on the power tied up under that National Forest. Power is where it's at, honey, and don't you forget it."

Rhonna didn't answer, but said to herself that power was always the issue for men like Ned, and probably for men like Cal, too. She began to understand what had drawn her to environmental causes. Trees were beautiful, usable throwaways, like women, at least in the eyes of power-driven men. Cal was right about that, anyway, even if he was driven by power of another sort. Against him, as against Ned, any tactics were justified, since the power was so one-sided in this fight that she had thrown herself into.

The Xlendi Hotel gathered in its guests like a light pulling in moths. Rhonna was glad for Ned's supporting arm, since the crowd that swarmed around her was straight out of the society pages. She recognized a royal face here, a movie star there. Her head was swimming in this unfamiliar element.

"Wait for me, Ned. I need to stop at the ladies' room." She went into the black and chrome art-deco lounge and stood for a moment with her head leaning back against the door.

When she opened her eyes, she saw Cristina Montani redundantly applying some eye shadow to her already mysterious dark eyes.

"Aren't you the one Cal rescued from my motor boat?" Cristina pouted, checking her bright red lips for smudges.

Rhonna wondered if Cal's kisses were the cause of a faint smear at one blurred corner of the Contessa's lush mouth. "I guess so. But don't let it spoil your night. I've got zero interest in Cal Conway. Almost married men are not in my line." She leaned over the rippled gray marble counter and inspected her naturally dark-lashed eyes, as if they might need mascara. She had no desire to look at Cal's countess.

"And you think Cal Conway is an almost married man?"

Cristina neatly erased the red blur with a corner of her tissue.

"Ned Peavey says so." Rhonna touched her lips with frosted coral and snapped the lipstick cover back on.

"And a man as rich as Ned is always right, *n'est pas*?" Cristina closed her formidable makeup kit and put it in her gold lamé bag.

"*Sans doute,*" Rhonna said politely, for the first time glad for her year of college French. "And if he has uranium for sale, he is more than right, *n'est-ce pas*? He is practically God."

Cristina paused before sweeping dramatically through the door in her black watered silk strapless gown. "And who are you to know he has uranium for sale? He tells no one his business."

Since the other woman was gone, Rhonna said out loud what she was thinking. "God knows, and God judges."

Alone, Rhonna stood for a moment with her hands in a prayer position before her face. "Reality check complete. Ned Peavey's selling uranium that belongs to the American government. Now, I've got to find out who he's selling it to."

She ran a brush quickly through her pale gold, waving hair, then self-confidently sailed out the door. Only a quick step backward saved her from slamming straight into the broad chest of Cal Conway.

"Cristina just let me know you think I'm not available. Is that right?" He held her firmly by her arms.

Rhonna tried to pull away. "You've got no right to fool around with my feelings, Cal. Or even to know what they are. It's not fair, not fair!" Tears were coming to her eyes and she wished furiously that Cal would free her hands so she could brush them away.

"You seem so sure I'm fooling around," Cal said in his steady voice, keeping his eyes on hers. "Believe me, I'm not." Music began to drift in from the nearby hall.

"How can I?" she whispered. "If you broke my heart, I think it would maybe kill me. I'm not about to let it happen."

Cal's answer was to take her in his arms and swirl her onto the dance floor, half lifting her off the ground as he buried his face in her neck. His lips moved against her throat, and she felt a rush of energy roll through her like thunder. Her body was charged with the fire from his, and she melted in his arms as they began to dance. She had slight experience of ballroom dancing, since she had preferred dancing alone, in private. But with Cal, no experience was necessary. He was a master of the art. She became part of him as he dipped her so low that the ends of her hair brushed the floor. Then he swung her against him as if she was a doll with no will of her own. *Not quite a doll, though,* Rhonna told herself, her head dizzy as she raised her face to his. For she felt more alive than ever in her life, as if she was complete for the first time, a cup overflowing. Her lips opened to speak, trembled, and no words came out.

He brushed his mouth lightly against hers and smiled down at her as they moved in slow circles. "Say it. Say you want me the way I want you." The muscle in his jaw worked a little and his mouth was tense. "It's time we said what we've been thinking ever since we laid eyes on each other."

"I can't, I can't want you," she burst out, tearing herself from his arms. "You don't understand. I'm a Christian, Cal. What I do with my body matters to me. To God. Just wanting isn't enough. There has to be loving, too. And that's not in your book of tricks, Cal."

"This gentleman giving you some trouble, pretty lady?"

Ned Peavey slipped his arms around her and swept her off in a fast polka. She had a glimpse or two of Cal leaning against the wall, his arms folded, watching her with a raised eyebrow. Then he vanished.

"You look good enough to serve for hors d'oeuvres," Ned murmured into her hair. "I've been watching you. When you're turned on, your face gets this beautiful shade of pink. I'd like to be the one to make that happen."

"I feel sick," Rhonna gasped, pushing him away. "Too much champagne." She had drunk nothing but ginger ale, but somehow felt as if she had something in her system that didn't belong there. She felt emotionally jerked around, whether by Cal, who sensed her weakness for him, or by Ned, who had seen it and wanted to use it to cash in on what Cal had roused in her.

Rhonna ran out onto the balcony, then slipped into the shadows where Ned could not find her. He came out looking, but gave up after a few minutes, perhaps going in search of the seductive contessa. *Good. Let him and Cal Conway fight over this woman who fascinates them both so much.* Rhonna tasted the salt of tears running down her cheeks and wished miserably that she were home in bed. If this was what it was like to be in love, she wanted no part of it. For she was in love with Cal Conway. It was about time she admitted the fact to herself, even if she could not admit it to Cal when he pressed her. Once he knew how she felt, he would never let up until he had her. *And he was close to his goal,* Rhonna said to herself, *let's admit that too, while we're in a soul-searching mode.* But she was still her own person, and would be as long as she could not be sure of this man who had so shaken her self-possession. Rhonna had to repeat the words three times before she even half believed them.

'I am still my own person,' she said softly, willing the words to be true. *I'm still Christ's own. My promise stands.* Voices were whispering near her and Rhonna shrank farther back into the shadows. Ned Peavey and Cristina Montani were standing close together in a small circle of light from a flower-decked lantern above them. Ned's fingertips were driving into Cristina's shapely, bare shoulders.

"Your father promised me the use of that Long Island land," he muttered. "Unrestricted use."

"Can I help it if the senator can't force the owner to sell? You'll just have to wait until the place is foreclosed." Cristina pulled her arm away and tossed her cloud of dark frizzed curls back over her shoulder. "My father's only an ambassador. There's a limit to what he can do."

"Then you won't mind if I take care of the senator my way?" Ned stood closer to the contessa, blowing smoke in her face. "Of course you won't expect to get paid any extra. Yacht fuel is getting expensive, I hear."

"And if I say I'll spill to Cal everything I know about the uranium deposits under the Adirondack national forests, won't that get me at least another million? Wouldn't he love to know you've already got a uranium contract with China and another coming up with North Korea?" Cristina purred. "I just love to talk to that man. It would take something big to make me keep quiet. Especially about that deal you've just about sewed up to privatize a hundred thousand acres. The one you said the President is about to sign? And the public knows nothing. Yet."

Ned twisted her arm behind her until she gasped. "And won't know. If you drop that tidbit to Cal Conway, you won't live to drop another. You hear me, Cristina? Stay on my ship, and you'll get somewhere. I took you up when your noble family didn't have a hundred euros in the bank. Remember that."

Cristina spat her words back at him, her carefully made-up face three inches from his. "All right. You have what you want. But in return I want a five percent interest in that Long Island resort you're planning. If you're picking up the best beach frontage in Southampton, I want some."

"And why would a cosmopolitan like you want a piece of a potato farm?"

"Cal's taken an interest in Southampton lately. We could enjoy it together."

"We'll call it a wedding gift." Ned let her arm go and dusted off his sleeves as if he might have caught something unpleasant from her.

Cristina laughed noncommittally and followed Ned back to the brilliantly lit hall.

Rhonna stepped out of the shadows and went over to lean on the railing. Her legs felt too weak to carry her. She held her cold hands to her flaming cheeks. Cal had to know about Cristina's plans to share her Long Island investment with him. Probably he had even guessed that the land was Rhonna's. *How many parcels of prime oceanfront land in Southampton are on the verge of being* foreclosed? *None that I know of.* And the two of them would vacation there, sipping their vintage wines while they watched the sun go down from their balcony, overlooking her beach.

The tears fell from her eyes and rolled between her fingers. *Bad enough to lose the farm, but it's worse even than that.* Cal had been playing with her, getting information about the place she loved, no doubt laughing with Cristina about the gullible little country girl he planned to have a week's fling with before settling down with his countess.

She wondered if Cal knew Cristina had been a penniless aristocrat before becoming Ned Peavey's mistress. Well, she said to herself, tossing her head so that the curving ends of her thick mane tickled her bare shoulders and back, it wasn't her business and she wouldn't be the one to gossip about Cristina's secret. If Cal wanted someone's throwaway, he could have the contessa. Probably he didn't care what sort of past the glamorous Cristina had, given his own.

"You look like a ship's figurehead, scanning the stars," Cal said softly, coming up behind her. He put his hands on the railing on either side of hers, so she was trapped.

Rhonna's cheeks turned hot again, and she turned so that her face was right under his, their bodies almost touching. The piney scent of him, his hard jaw with the dark bristles beginning to show on it, the glint of his narrowed eyes as he looked down at her made her unsteady. She wanted to tell him she despised him, that she knew all about what he was planning with Cristina, that he was not the man God meant for her. Couldn't be. Not with his track record.

But somehow, with the moonlight turning his auburn hair bright, and his breath warming her forehead, all she wanted to do was melt against him and let him do whatever he liked with her. Rhonna took a deep breath and tried to clear her head. He was waiting for her to do just that, to let him have her without a struggle. The slight smile on his face frightened her, for she supposed it meant that turning her to melted butter was a joke, one which she was sure he would tell Cristina someday, probably when they were summering in Southampton. She stiffened, leaning against the rail.

"A figurehead's made of wood," she retorted. "No feelings. Wasn't it Hemingway who said his idea of the perfect woman was one who was blind and dumb? Your favorite writer, as I recall."

"For his style," Cal said, tipping her chin up so she had to meet his eyes steadily. "Not for his opinions."

He stood closer, just close enough that his body brushed hers. Rhonna felt the familiar electricity shoot through her body making her tremble. She wrapped her scarf around her as if she was only cold, not struck to the heart by her longing for this man to take her in his arms and hold her until she was breathless, half-conscious, unable to remember that he belonged to someone else.

"And for you, I suppose, style is everything," she murmured. "For me, it's content that matters. The truth."

He ignored her words and ran one fingertip lightly over her lips. "God, Rhonna, I think I would give the rest of my life to spend one night next to you, catching the breath as it leaves your mouth, feeling every inch of your body moving against mine, skin to skin. I've actually prayed for that, would you believe." Suddenly his face blotted out the moon and the stubble on his jaw scraped her skin as he ground his lips into hers, pulling her up against him so hard she lost her breath.

She let herself go limp against him, hardly moving her arms to hold him, for she felt her will draining out of her as her body surged against his. She forgot everything she hated about Cal Conway and knew only that she loved and wanted him as if her life depended on her body merging with his. She let her head fall back against his encircling arm, let her mouth open against his, and did not care that his hot hands were running all over her, as if memorizing her curves.

"I've got a friend's sailboat at the dock," he whispered against her ear, his breath tickling her flesh until she moaned. "Let's forget about the others and go back together. I want to hold you all night. God, woman, I want to drown in you and that's the truth."

"Don't let's talk about truth, just now," Rhonna sighed, letting him half carry her down the stone steps toward the dock. "Your truth and mine are different. I wish I was going home with you, yes. But to *our* home, not a hotel."

For the next hour, bundled into Cal's jacket, Rhonna lay back against the side of the little sailboat, her legs wedged tightly against his, watching him guide the little craft surely across the sparkling water. He must have liked the feel of her bare legs next to him, for he was careful not to move away, even as he had to stretch his lean length to bring the ship about in order to avoid the rocks between Gozo and Malta. She watched dreamily as he crouched over her, avoiding the boom as it swung over them both, watched as the muscles of his chest and arms rippled under the gauze-thin, tightly fitted dress shirt, which he had pulled open at the neck.

When they stood outside her hotel room door, Rhonna found her hands were shaking too much to put the key in the lock. She looked up at Cal, mutely appealing for a rescue. In a moment he had the door open and closed it behind it when they entered. He tossed his jacket across the chair, then moved toward her, his arms around her before she could back away. He whirled her around as he had on the dance floor and smiled down into her face, laced with light from the moon that shone in the window.

"I would like to be able to tell you more than I have, Rhonna,' he said, letting her go suddenly. "More about myself. You talked about truth, before. I need to be straight with you."

He must be thinking about Cristina, she thought, *about their marriage plans.* Rhonna's heart hardened. She had not wanted to be reminded, had wanted to stay in the enchantment of the moment, not thinking about tomorrow and Cristina's laughing shrug as she pulled him off to her yacht for a spin to Monte Carlo or wherever such people went for their weekends. Southampton was one such place. Somehow that picture killed her excitement, leaving her cold and numb.

"It's no good," she said flatly. "You're out of my league, and I'd better get used to it. Tonight was lovely, like a good movie. But that's all it could be."

Cal's long lips hardened in a tight line. "Your trouble is, you think too much," he said. "I'd rather you saved thinking for the last conference session, tomorrow. Your friend Ned is going to push the delegates to vote against banning private exploitation of government land around the world."

"You didn't tell me that before," Rhonna watched him nervously as he looked down at her computer table. On it, neatly piled, were her notes, which she had printed in the hotel office that afternoon. "No, don't. That's private," she cried out, as he picked up the first page.

He held her off with one hand as he read, his heavy dark brows pulled together over the hawk-like arch of his nose. "Very nice, Rhonna, very nice," he said tossing the paper on the desk and brushing her hand from his arm. "As always, you write like a pro."

He picked up the fax cover sheet lying beside the notes and inspected it. "I see you're working for *Newstar*. A double agent. You had me fooled."

"I didn't take anything of yours," she cried, her eyes suddenly stinging with tears. "And you never asked me if I was a journalist."

"And you never asked me if I was going to marry Cristina Montani." Cal threw his jacket over his shoulder and opened the door. "For investigative reporters, the two of us leave a lot to be desired."

"I have one more day to work for you," Rhonna said, trying to keep her voice steady, while her hands twisted in the rainbow chiffon of her skirt. "I'll put in my time. It would be good to help pass the ban."

"Okay." He gave her a long look up and down, as if he was painting her into his memory. "A truce, then, for tomorrow. I'll give you a list of delegates who're wavering. You talk to the first half, I'll talk to the rest. Good night, Rhonna."

As always, when he said her name it was as though he was caressing it. Even when Cal was angry with her, the name came out gently. He walked outside into the hall, almost closed the door, paused a moment, then clicked it shut behind him.

Rhonna walked over to the desk and picked up the pile of papers. This afternoon, she had been so proud of them. The detail was comprehensive and accurate, and human interest stories warmed every other paragraph. Her grasp of the issues, Bill Kingsley would say, beaming at her from over his tiny reading glasses, did him proud. Still, for a moment she had the urge to take the whole pile next door, apologize to Cal, and throw all her work in his shredder. She had never before betrayed a trust, and it hurt her to the heart that she had betrayed Cal's, for however good a reason, even if he had been lying to her about Cristina.

Not now, she said sensibly to herself, hanging up her dress, splashing water on her face, and falling into bed. *Tomorrow will be soon enough.* That night she dreamed of her father sitting at the kitchen table, his hands over his face. *He can't take one more loss. First mother, now the farm.* When Rhonna woke up the next day, she knew what she had to do, and it wasn't to throw away her stories. They were hers, and if Cal Conway thought less of her for what she had done, that was his problem. The land would be there for her long after he would, with his easy kisses and easy goodbys.

Chapter Five

The next morning, Rhonna put on her periwinkle blue linen suit, sprayed some lemony cologne over her shining, freshly brushed hair, and picked up her notebook. She hoped she looked more businesslike than she felt. When she joined Cal in the hall, after his light knock, she didn't look up at him. Matching her steps as best she could to his long ones, she kept her eyes straight ahead.

"I had a dream about you just as I was waking up," Cal said, his voice remote, as if he was recounting the morning news. "Thought you were next to me, but I was just squeezing the life out of my pillow. Have you ever before had a pillow mistaken for you?"

"Not that I know of." Rhonna didn't look up. "I'm not responsible for what happens in my own dreams, let alone other people's."

"We agreed on a truce, remember?" Cal opened the door to the dining room. "I won't bite your head off, if you promise the same."

"Okay." Rhonna managed a half smile. "Let's see that list of names. We'd better start early if we're going to block that vote."

An hour later, by the time the last conference was about to begin, Rhonna and Cal met at the main door. They stood close together, his head bent over hers. We stood just this way last night when we were about to kiss, she thought, but now it was only business. At least for him, she was sure. As for her, she still felt a tingle of excitement shoot through her as his hand touched hers, and she had to lean against the wall to seem casual.

"I think I got four out of six," she said coolly. "How'd you do?"

His voice was carefully distanced, but he kept his eyes on hers and she could feel their heat go straight into her, turning her insides warm. "Five, maybe. Richon, from France, won't say what he's going to do. Has to phone home for instructions, he says, *s'il vous plaît*."

Cal mimicked the waffling little Frenchman's nervous manner and Rhonna had to laugh.

"I wasn't sure," Cal said, "whether he needed to call his government or his mother."

At that, Rhonna's tension broke, and she laughed until the tears came to her eyes. "At least he didn't invite you home to *meet* his mother. That's what the Argentinian delegate did to me!" she said, wiping her palm across her damp eyes.

Cal smiled a little and took her hand, quickly kissing it on the inside of the wrist. She felt his tongue touch for a moment, and her whole body contracted as if he had crushed her in his arms.

"If I took you home, Rhonna," he said softly, looking into her eyes, "it wouldn't be to meet my mother. I'd want you all to myself."

Rhonna was about to answer him that he'd have a lot of explaining to do, since his mother could hardly mistake her for an Italian contessa. But Ned Peavey came up and stood between Rhonna and Cal, his broad back to her.

"I hear you've been sucking up votes for the ban," he spat out. "Just watch it, Conway. I can have you taken out any time you get too busy."

He turned and looked Rhonna up and down as if she was an exotic entrée he meant to tear into. "Why don't you quit working for this guy? If he keeps on doing what he's doing, he's going to wind up ground meat."

Ned charged into the conference room, leaving a spicy perfume odor behind him.

"He's running scared," Cal said calmly, taking her by the elbow to lead her to their press seats. "Ned always turns bully when he's losing."

As the delegates spoke for and against the resolution to ban private exploitation of government land, Rhonna tracked the yes votes in her notebook. Her heart pounded as the time to vote approached.

"I counted 72 for the ban and 55 against," she whispered to Cal, leaning so close to his ear that when his face suddenly turned to her, her lips brushed against his cheek. She blushed and took a deep breath, hoping he would not hear her heart pound. "Looking good."

"They can talk one way for the press and vote another," Cal replied, keeping his mouth close to hers.

"Then we could still lose." Rhonna's face fell.

Cal blew gently on her hot forehead and smiled. "And stagger off to fight another day. If you'd lost as many as I have over the years, Rhonna, you'd yawn at this one."

"I hear you've won a lot too," she said, thinking of how easily he had almost won her.

"Only when I set my mind to it," he answered, his mouth unsmiling now, his jaw hard. "You haven't begun to see what I'm capable of."

There was a brief recess before the vote and Cal began to move among the delegates, his tall, taut body relaxing into one conversation after another. All the delegates seemed to know him and listened with serious faces as he spoke, then moved on to someone else. Even Richon, the nervous little Frenchman stepped over to him and bowed politely. Rhonna couldn't be sure what the Frenchman was saying, but from Cal's smile, she assumed Richon was saying yes.

"I've done what I can," Cal said, dropping back into the chair as the voting began. "Look at Ned over there. He's sweating like a hunk of lard in a chicken coop."

Rhonna turned to him suddenly. "Funny you should say that. My father used to say it, too."

"You didn't know I grew up on a farm in southern Vermont, did you?" Cal said, with a teasing edge to his voice. "That was before my family sold our land and got into corporate stocks. So much the worse for them." He shrugged his broad shoulders. "My official bio doesn't tell it all."

"No, I didn't know that." Rhonna's voice was low and her eyes were on his roughly chiseled profile. "So you don't think low of farm folks?"

"I've come a long way from my roots," he said enigmatically, and his hand gripped her arm. "Look, they've finished the count."

"Sixty-nine for," the spokesman read off his paper, "and fifty-eight against. The delegates have passed by nine votes Resolution 103, a complete ban on private use of government lands for purposes of mining or logging."

Rhonna and Cal leaped to their feet cheering, and he slapped his hand overhead against hers in victory.

"I owe you one, Conway," Peavey growled as he stamped by them, hardly glancing to either side.

"And I've owed you one, Ned, for a long time," Cal said softly, half to himself. Then he turned to Rhonna again.

"I told you how much I like to win," Cal said, putting his arms around her, at the waist and shoulders. "Now you know."

A discreet gloved hand tapped her on the shoulder and Cal let go. "Telegram for you, Miss Moran. From the U.S.A. Southhampton, it says."

If someone was trying to reach her, they might have used her cell phone, Rhonna thought, then realized that in her hurry, she had left it in her room.

Cal took the envelope and shoved it in his pocket. "Later," he said. "Right now I've ordered us a lunch and some victory champagne to be brought to our balcony. We've got a lot to celebrate."

"You're not mad anymore about my story for *Newstar*?" Rhonna let herself be propelled toward the elevator. She wanted to pull her telegram out of Cal's pocket, but felt overcome by a sudden loss of nerve. Just being so close to him melted all her resolve and drew her into the moment so intensely and totally that her mind could handle no more than the waves of warm honey pouring through her body at that moment. Everything else vanished out of her head.

"After what I've pulled to get stories in my time?" Cal laughed low in his throat and half-lifted her against him as they squeezed into the crowded elevator. "Once I pretended to be from the Department of the Interior and walked into the corporate file room of the country's biggest chemical manufacturer. That's how the Buffalo Canal story broke. They'd been killing people for years with the junk they were dropping into that water."

"You were lucky they didn't kill you," Rhonna said, thinking of Ned's threat.

"Oh, they tried." Cal got out his keys and opened her door, one arm still tightly around her. "But I got the goods on their top executive. Made friends with his secretary."

Rhonna felt her heart chill at the words. The chasm between his expediency and her Christianity widened so abruptly she stopped walking forward. "That's how you nailed the friends of your family who were head over heels into pollution, isn't it?" Her voice was cool, and he picked up her aloofness instantly.

"You use what you have to when the odds are against you and the stakes are high enough." Cal opened the door to the balcony, then swung her across the room in a sweeping, circular dance step until she stood at his side, looking at the harbor view. "Surely you, of all people, know that?"

Rhonna blushed, remembering the night before. She was remembering more than his discovery of her story. The kiss on the hotel balcony at the party, the sailboat trip home, and the sense she had had of being out of her own control, ready to move with him like a sail in the wind. She felt her breath tearing through her throat. She let her head fall back and looked into his dark eyes which were fiercely staring into hers. He held her close with one hand, then reached around her with the other, picking up the telephone by the bed.

"Cancel that lunch order for room 312," he said, his voice gravelly and slow. "I'll let you know later."

"Lunch is a better idea, Cal," Rhonna said, hardly able to get out the words, her heart was pounding so fast.

"I've waited for this, for you, all my life," he whispered, his hands on the top button of her blouse. "You can't know how much I've wanted you."

The phone rang and Rhonna's hand groped for it before Cal could stop her. She hung onto the receiver with both hands. "Megan? How did you where to find me?" Rhonna fought to keep from sounding like she was doing what she was doing.

"Bill Kingsley told me the name of the hotel. Why didn't you answer your cell phone? I had to send a telegram." Megan's voice was high-pitched and strident, as she used to sound when she was on diet pills. "Rhonna, your father needs you. Another heart attack. He's in intensive care. You've got to come home. Now."

"I'm out of here." Rhonna pushed Cal away, feeling foolish to be in the arms of a virtual stranger while her father might be dying. "I'll call you from Kennedy as soon as I get in." She hung up, gasping as if she had been pulled from underwater. *Lord, I know you were stopping me just in time. But please, save my father's life. Take care of him for me.*

Cal had turned the phone slightly and was listening too. He took the receiver out of her hand and hung up.

"I thought this was too good to be true," he said, pulling her to her feet, his fingers cool against the heat of her bare arms. "It's not a good time to ask for a rain check, but I'm asking." Rhonna began to hurry around the room, throwing things into her bag.

"No, it's not a good time," she said, brushing away the tears running down her cheeks. "The worst, in fact." She slung the bag over her shoulder and started out the door.

"You'd better go now," she said shakily. "I don't seem to function well when you're around."

"Oh yes, you do," Cal said softly, kissing her on the tip of her slightly turned-up nose. "You function supremely well. I'll go and make some arrangements. Wait."

He vanished down the hall and Rhonna pulled herself together, her hands shaking so that she could hardly manage the button that had come apart so easily under Cal's skilled fingers. All the while she was in Cal's arms, her father had been struggling for breath, his chest crushed in the killing clamp of heart failure, as he longed for her to be with him. *And here I was thinking only of myself and Cal,* she thought, *of wanting him close to me.* Slipping on her jacket and looking around the room for any last, forgotten item, she could still feel the heat of his body. It would be a funny story for her father, she thought wryly, not bothering to lock the door behind her, if only he was alive to hear it when she got to the hospital.

She ran into Ned Peavey checking out at the registration desk.

"I heard you had a telegram," he said, his face all sympathy. "Hope you don't mind that I had the clerk read it to me."

"Of course I mind," Rhonna snapped, remembering that this was the man who had threatened to kill Cal for getting the ban passed. "What would you expect?"

"I'd expect you want to get home as fast as you can," Ned said smoothly, slipping his hand under her arm. "The next commercial flight out doesn't leave until tomorrow morning. I've checked." "No!" Rhonna turned her head toward him fast, her hair flying into her eyes. "Dad may be dead by then. I've got to get back tonight."

"Then you'd better go with me. My jet is waiting on the landing strip. I'll have you in Southampton by six PM."

"I have to tell Cal first," she said, desperately pulling away. "He's making arrangements for me."

"Your choice." Ned shrugged. "I'm leaving now." Rhonna ran after him, her bag flopping against her hip.

"Just a minute. At least I have to leave a message with the clerk." She hated imagining Cal's furious scowl when he found that she had left with Ned and not waited as he had asked. But she hated even more the thought of her father slipping out of life without her beside him. *It's a sacrifice I can't make, not even for Cal. Not even if it means I'll never see him again.*

Ned wasn't stopping. He wasn't about to give her time to leave a message.

"Okay, I'm coming," she called to Ned, and ran across the tiled floor, her high heels clicking like a metronome. "You win."

As the words were out of her mouth and she reached his side, she turned around for a last glance at the hotel, and saw Cal standing at the desk staring at her, his face dark with fury, his fist clenched on the counter as the clerk leaned toward him. Then Ned pulled her out the door into his waiting car, and they were on their way to the airport.

Cal stood at the hotel door, his eyes following the car that carried Rhonna off with Ned. No taxi was in sight, or he would have followed them and stopped her at the airport. Too bad he'd already turned in his rental car. An unfamiliar sense of frustration filled him, and he felt the urge to slam his head against the glass. His body felt leaden, as if she had taken all the life in it away with her. Strange, how alive he had felt just a few minutes before, holding her, seeing the pink flush spread across her delicate face, feeling the soft skin warm under his fingers. *Damn, but this woman drives me crazy.* One minute, flowing through him like music, the next running off on some scheme of her own, forgetting him.

He leaned his hot forehead against the cool glass of the door and closed his eyes. Long ago, his mother had said to him that he would get his comeuppance someday for the way he dumped women and took off for parts unknown, on some compelling assignment that made him forget everything but the present moment. Comeuppance. He smiled grimly at the old-fashioned word that was so characteristic of Ellen Conway, with her lace tablecloths and church meetings. How had she ever spawned a son like him, whose idea of home was someone else's hotel room in Paris? She had said he was like her at heart, wanting to give love, not just take it, but until now, he had been dead sure she was wrong.

Just at this moment, when he felt ready to give more love than he had ever known was in him, Rhonna had taken off with a savage who would cheerfully cook his own grandmother for dinner. Rhonna would be alone with Ned Peavey on his jet for time enough that he could do anything he liked with her. Cristina had told him that Ned's pilot and valet had been instructed to keep the cockpit door closed and not answer any calls for help. Cal remembered Cristina laughing as she said that any woman who put herself in Ned's hands deserved whatever she got. But not Rhonna, not Rhonna, Cal repeated in a low, distracted voice. He didn't believe she had gone with Ned for any other reason but her father's need of her. Rhonna's body had not lied to him. He knew women well enough to know that. She was in that plane only to get home fast. The trouble was, Ned was twice her size. Cal strode over to the desk, his hands curled as if he planned to knock the clerk against the wall.

The little man cowered as Cal approached, misreading the expression on the tall American's face. "There's a fax for you, Mr. Conway. Right here."

Cal snatched it up. Before reading, he gave his credit card to the clerk. "Take care of my bill. And call the number on this paper to confirm the private flight I ordered. I'll be leaving on it alone."

It was a flight Rhonna should have been on with me, he thought bitterly, turning away from the desk as he read the fax. Perhaps she would have been, had he explained to her that his "arrangements" included chartering a plane to take them home. He had been too sure that she would leave the plans to him. Hadn't he seen in her that same wild, impulsive streak he knew in himself? Of course she would handle her own arrangements. *I should have seen it coming. And she has no reason to think I have that kind of money.* Thanks to his mother's generosity, her half of the family's assets was already in his name. He would have been happy to spend thousands more to ensure that Rhonna would have a chance to see her father alive. Yet he had not told her that, wanting her trust and gambling on the hope that she would give it.

Cal felt an emptiness opening inside him that he had not felt since childhood. He had lost his faith early, sure that he needed no help managing his life. Certainly no help from a God he couldn't see or feel, as he had explained to his mother. She had cried and prayed, but still he had gone his own way, only vaguely aware of a God-shaped hole in his heart that hurt unless he was on a romantic or journalistic hunt. Afterward the restlessness would set in, the sense that his life had no meaning apart from his appetites. He remembered the way Rhonna's slight form melted against his and the aliveness of her pale golden hair under his hands. T*he two of us aren't finished,* he told himself, *not by a long shot. We haven't even begun.* The first thing he would do when he got home was to find Rhonna. The second, he decided, surprising himself, was to call his mother. He wanted to tell her about Rhonna, though he had no idea what he would say.

Cal walked up the steps to his room, reading as he went. The fax was from the AP office, acknowledging receipt of his story. At the request of someone calling from higher up, they had sent the story out to second-string papers as well as the major ones. Now, who would have bothered to make sure papers like Rhonna's would get his story? Cal crushed the fax into a ball and shoved it in his pocket. Rhonna's paper. *They'll bump her story for mine, and she'll think I did it. Didn't I tell her I'd do anything for a story? Anything to get what I want? Here I was, hoping she'd know I meant her. That I would do anything to have her.* "And I would," he said softly to himself, "I would."

Opening the door to the room she had just left, Cal looked at her rumpled bed. He walked across the room and ran his hand over the pillow where her head had lain, hoping he might find a strand of hair. But there was nothing. The room was as lonely and sterile as the hundreds of hotels he had stayed in. Cal stood at the window, looking out over the harbor. The view did not seem so exotic and desirable to him now.

For the first time since his family had sold their farm in Vermont, he felt himself longing to go home. A phone rang insistently in the next room. Knowing it was Cristina, Cal did not hurry to answer. *I don't deserve Rhonna,* he said to himself. *Cristina's the kind I'm likely to wind up with, God help me.* The words came out unexpectedly. Cal felt embarrassed, as if he had been caught talking to himself like some lonely street person. His mother had told him that people talked to whatever god they loved. And his god had been himself, Cal admitted. He had created a clay-footed god out of his own driven ego, and losing Rhonna was no more than he deserved. Still, he tried to pray, for her sake. *God, help her. Don't let Ned hurt her the way he hurt my sister.*

Now that he had her to himself, Ned was all sweet concern, insisting on carrying her bag into the sleek living room of his Lear jet. By the time the plane was cleared for take-off, he had her sitting on the leather couch, with her feet up on the chrome and glass coffee table, pretending to sip a margarita so potent that just the smell of it made her feel slightly smashed. Ned had put on a paisley printed smoking jacket and poured himself a drink before sitting down across the table from her.

Rhonna could see the flat Maltese landscape whipping by the window as the plane rolled down the runway, then the shore of the island, pale against the ripples of blue sea. Cal was down there somewhere, she thought, hating herself for being with Ned, for walking away from Cal when he was trying to help, leaving him to think she believed his help wasn't as good as Ned's. *Well, in this case it wasn't,* Rhonna said to herself, trying to be reasonable.

A day's wait might mean she would never see her father alive again. *If Cal can't understand that, it's because he wants to think the worst of me.* He had certainly jumped to damaging conclusions the night before, assuming she had stolen his material for her own story. Trust seemed a big thing with him, almost as big as it was for her. Yet both of them had betrayed each other—he by being an uncommitted man and she by taking his job offer under false pretenses. Neither had any right to blame the other, Rhonna thought, but still she blamed Cal. It was easier than blaming herself, which she felt inclined to do, after letting that telegram stay in Cal's pocket.

Ned was leaning toward her across the narrow glass table, and Rhonna suddenly woke up from her daydream of Cal. She realized that she had six hours to kill with this predatory man, who was strong and mean enough to do anything he wanted at thirty thousand feet above the Atlantic, and no one would be there to stop him. Rhonna felt the sweat beginning to trickle from under her loose, windswept hair. No wonder Cal had been so angry at seeing her leave with Ned. He figured she knew what she was in for and was willing.

She got up and freshened Ned's half-gone drink with a generous amount of tequila from the bar. At the same time, she dumped her margarita in the sink and replaced it with juice.

"What did Cal mean about you owing him one? Anything to do with Cristina?" She sat down opposite him in a padded leather recliner, keeping her feet firmly on the floor and her spine straight. Ned might interpret kicking back as a sign of weakness.

"You care a lot about what Conway thinks, don't you?" Ned didn't answer directly, but tossed half his drink down in one gulp.

"I'm just trying to figure him out," she said, swirling her drink around and staring into it. A plan was forming in her mind, and she eyed the tequila bottle on the bar, wondering when the best time was for her to give Ned some more.

"You don't have to look far for his motives," Ned said between clenched teeth. "The man's a spoiler. Whether it's with a woman or someone else's business plans, Cal Conway steps on toes. Especially mine."

"You think he's after you in particular?" Rhonna raised one eyebrow. The man was paranoid into the bargain. She was on a plane with a sex-crazed paranoiac who was out to get revenge on Cal. What better way could he find than to attack the woman Cal had obviously been after? The sweat was now running down Rhonna's back and she shivered a little as a blast from the plane's air-conditioning caught her. She got up and poured margarita mix and tequila into Ned's glass in equal portions, not bothering with ice. The less diluted his drinks were, the faster he might pass out. *Of course*, she realized, *he may get crazy when he's drunk. This gambit could go either way.* She would just have to trust in God and use a heavy hand with the tequila.

"He has reason to be." Ned's tongue slurred a little, and he hiccupped. "Ten years ago his sister came up against me in a land suit. She had kept twenty acres of the family's Vermont land. I guess he told you his family once owned anything worth skiing on around Stowe? No? Well, I'm telling you now." He paused and stared into space, his small, narrow eyes vacant.

"Okay, so he had a sister," Rhonna prompted, keeping her fingers around the neck of the tequila bottle. "What happened to her?"

Ned put his feet on the couch and lay back, staring at the ceiling. "She borrowed on the land to pay the taxes and couldn't pay back the loan."

"Why didn't she ask the family for money? Why didn't she ask Cal?" Rhonna probed, trying to imagine this sister of Cal's who sounded so much like herself.

"Nancy was proud, like him. It had been her idea to hang onto a piece of the family land. Thought she could make a go of a flower stand or some damned thing. Stupid of her. No growing season worth talking about in Vermont." Ned snorted and held out his glass, which Rhonna filled again, this time pouring in more tequila than mix.

"What was she like?" Rhonna's hands were trembling so that she almost upset the bottle when she put it on the floor beside her.

"Pretty, except for this habit she had of frowning all the time. Wouldn't put out. As you can imagine, I tried to change her mind." His glass clinked hard against his teeth, as if he'd misjudged the distance between the two. "Tough, I guess you'd call Nancy. Funny she went in for flowers. I offered her a break, but she wouldn't take it."

"There was a price to the loan?" Rhonna kept her voice light and innocent. All the while she was thinking, *so this is what men without God are like, worse than wild animals.*

"Oh yes, there's always a price. Right, honey?" Ned turned and leered at her. "You better believe there's a price. I don't do good deeds to save my soul. Man, you have pretty legs. Conway ever tell you that?"

Rhonna shivered again and slipped more tequila, straight this time, into Ned's glass. "So you made a deal with Cal's sister. What did she do?"

"Nancy tried to get the foreclosure sale stopped." Ned's words ran into each other and he almost dropped his drink. "When she couldn't, she shot herself in the head. That was when the family found out about the money she owed me."

Rhonna wanted to cry, to strangle this man, to break the bottle over his nose. Cal's sister, a woman who loved the land as she did, pushed to the brink of death and finally over it. She felt tears rising and a pain in her that couldn't make its way out except by screams. It was not a time for screaming, she thought, holding one hand to her throat.

"I see," she said, seeing Nancy, seeing the whole bloody, life-smashing thing Ned had done to Cal's sister. "And what did Cal do about it?"

Ned laughed, hiccupping again and holding out his glass for her to fill. Apparently he didn't care how drunk he got. "He came after me with his bare fists. My goons held him off. Now he comes after me in other ways." Ned sat up shakily.

Rhonna mechanically poured the rest of the bottle into his glass, and he slugged it down. She felt the same pain Cal's sister Nancy must have felt, heart contracting, eyes hot and burning, pain deep in the gut where life either took hold or petered out. For Nancy, it had gone out like a light.

"Cal said you'd killed her," she whispered.

"That's what he thought." Ned stood up and walked carefully around the table until he stood next to her. Then he wound his arms around Rhonna and put his lips against her forehead, letting them slide wetly down her face. "So what do you think, gorgeous one, you blaze in blue? How about you and me not wasting any more time?"

Rhonna put up her hands between her body and his, then shoved him backward, flat on the floor. He lay there, mouth open and eyes closed, making a noise like an idling truck. With luck, she thought, he'd be out until they landed in Southampton.

For the rest of the flight, Rhonna prayed for her father and read the tiny New Testament volume she carried in her purse. *O dear Jesus, I know I'm bargaining with you. I know it, but please, let my father live. And I'll marry nobody but a Christian.* Trying and failing to imagine Cal being baptized by Pastor Ken, Rhonna almost wished she could take her promise back. *I'm a Promise Keeper,* she reminded herself. *I won't let Cal tempt me again*

Chapter Six

By the time Ned Peavey came to, the plane was due to land in an hour, and Rhonna spent the time locked in the bathroom, reading *Fortune Magazine*, learning how to get rich. Ned pounded on the door, but she stuck her fingers in her ears and went on finding out more than she ever wanted to know about growth stocks in Europe. Once the plane had skidded to a stop on the wet runway of Southampton's little airport, she opened the bathroom door. Ned was lying on the couch with an ice bag on his forehead. He made a feeble gesture in her direction, then his hand fell back to the couch.

"You laid one on me," he said, not sounding as mad as she thought he would. "I should have known better."

"Thanks for the trip." Rhonna tossed her return ticket on the coffee table. "You can turn this in for cash. We're even."

Ned sat up, wincing, and watched her slide open the door hatch. "Not by a long shot," he said. "You'll hear from me, Rhonna Moran."

Something in his tone made Rhonna shiver as she tapped down the metal stairs pushed into place by the airport service workers. She didn't look back, but ran all the way to the terminal entrance, her bag bumping hard against her hip. Megan had left a message for her to taxi to the Suffolk County Hospital, where she would join her as soon as Rhonna called the *Newstar* office. Rhonna made two calls on her cell phone, one to the hospital's cardiac unit, and the other to *Newstar*. Since her father was sleeping under heavy sedation, she decided to stop first at *Newstar* to give her story to Bill Kingsley.

Her pick-up truck was still in the corner of the parking lot, and she dropped off her bag in the front seat. A pair of scuffed old beach sandals were under the seat and she put them on, glad to ditch the high heels. Cal wouldn't be there to see her anyway, and Rhonna didn't care what anyone else thought about how she looked. The warm late afternoon sun made her suit jacket unnecessary, and she tossed it in the truck on top of the bag. Walking into the building, she glanced through the pages of her story, glad to see it was as good as she thought it was, back on Malta. Good as Cal thought it was. At the mental image that came to her when she remembered Cal's anger as he looked through these same pages, Rhonna lost interest in reading anymore. He had thought she was a good writer. That was all she wanted to remember, not the sudden barrier that had risen between them when he felt she had betrayed him.

Bill Kingsley was at his desk scanning a long fax that was still coming off the roller. When she came in and tossed her story on the desk, he looked up. Something in his expression made her feel cold inside, and she sat down, waiting.

"Sorry about your Dad, babe," he said, raising his voice over the clicking and rumbling of the fax machine. "That's not all I'm sorry about. Glad you're sitting down."

Rhonna clutched her purse to keep her hands from shaking. "Go ahead. What's happened?"

"We just had a story on the Malta Conference come over the AP wires. Damn lucky to get it, too. I'm going to have to use it instead of yours, Rhonna."

Her shoulders dropped and she felt her whole body grow so limp she needed to lean back in her chair. "Don't tell me," she said in a shaky voice, "Cal Conway's story?"

"You got it." Bill's tone was kind, but businesslike. "I have no choice, Rhonna. You know that. It isn't everyday a little regional paper gets to run a story by Cal Conway."

"So I get nothing for what I wrote?" Rhonna's whole world was dropping around her in small, jagged pieces. She was too numb to cry or rage. Anyway, it wasn't Bill's fault. He had caved in to pressure, the way he always did. No use blaming him. It was Cal who had done this. Hadn't he said he'd do anything to get what he wanted? Right now, he probably wanted revenge and knew the best way to get it. With one move, he had checkmated her. *No story, no money, no tax payment. In his own way, Cal was as ruthless as Ned Peavey,* Rhonna told herself. She had been a fool to imagine otherwise.

Bill peered at her kindly over the cheaters that hung halfway down the bridge of his nose. "I can swing five hundred for your week's pay, but that's all, Rhonna. I'm sorry as I can be about this."

"I know you are." Rhonna wearily got up, feeling like her heart was too heavy for her body to carry. "Read the story anyhow. I'd like to know what you think of it."

Megan caught up with her on the way out to the parking lot, and her arms folded around Rhonna in a giant hug. Rhonna put her head down on Megan's plump, motherly shoulder and finally allowed a few tears to come.

"Great to see you, honey," Megan said, patting Rhonna's hair. "I hope you haven't been running around Malta in those awful shoes."

"Might as well have," Rhonna said, lifting her head so she wouldn't sniffle onto Megan's elegant silk jacket. "No story. A heavy hitter sent his in over the fax. Bumped mine." She wanted to say that she was in love with the heavy hitter, but hoped she could let that wait until she could say Cal's name without swearing or sobbing. "Bill's giving me my week's salary, but that barely covers the cost of the clothes. Megan, I'm destroyed. It's that simple."

"Oh, honey," Megan said, her pleasant, round face crumpling as if she were about to cry too. "I feel so bad. What a bummer. Let me take you to the hospital at least. You can tell me about it."

Rhonna poured out her whole story while Megan drove, crying as she had known would happen when the words brought back Cal's presence. She didn't mention Cristina's name, figuring Megan's elegant society mother probably knew her.

For Rhonna, words had always had the power to recreate the whole scene, with all the original feelings in high gear. She relived the look and feel of him, the scent of her pillow when his head had been on it, the touch of his hands running over her skin. *Lord, it's so hard to let him go,* she prayed, *help me not to* care.

"I wanted him so much, Megan," she wept, using up the last of her friend's tissues. "How am I going to put the pieces back together?"

"Well, start with doing your face," Megan said practically. "If your father's awake, he's going to need you to look cheerful. This Conway guy sounds like a charming stinker, just the kind we've always sworn we wouldn't be into."

"He is. I won't." Rhonna took some deep breaths, trying to mean her words. "It's behind me now. Looks like the farm is too. I wish I could lie to Dad about that, but he'd see right through me. Always does."

Megan sat in the waiting room while Rhonna went into the intensive care unit to see if her father was awake yet. Her legs felt weak when she saw him with tubes up his short, wide nose and an IV plugged into one arm. Electrodes were taped to his broad, hairy chest and were apparently responsible for the blips racing along a line on the monitor. The machines showed more life than he did. As soon as she said his name, Moran's eyes opened, and he winked at her.

"Dad! You're awake." she said, her voice catching in her throat. She had not realized how scared she had been. "They told me you were out cold."

"That's what they thought. I decided to play dead until you got here." Moran smiled at his daughter. "Nothing I wanted to say to them. How was the trip?"

"Pretty good. The temples were something else. I'll tell you later when you're up to seeing some postcards. But how about you?" Rhonna's hand crept up to his cheek slowly, trying to avoid the tangle of tubes and wires.

"I died, so they say. Saw the tunnel, the light, the whole near-death show. It was terrific," he laughed a little, then turned pale and was quiet a moment. "If it wasn't for you, Chipmunk, I'd have never come back. When they say God is beautiful, they aren't kidding. But I told myself and the angels up there, I'm going back to see my little girl get married."

"Then you'll have to stay in the land of the living for quite a while, Dad," Rhonna smiled at the pet name he'd called her ever since he caught her, as a small child, hiding her uneaten vegetables in her bureau drawer.

"I'm still waiting for the man who can replace you. For a minute or two, I thought I'd found him, but he let me down." She didn't mention that Cal might be feeling the same way about her.

Moran caught her hand in a grip that was still strong and stared into her eyes intently. "Now you listen. One of these days, I'm going to be long gone for the tall timber. I want to see you happy with a good Christian man. Maybe a kid or two."

"I'd be just as happy living on the farm by myself, Dad," Rhonna said, feeling a tightness in her chest when she thought of how happy he would have been if she'd come back with a man like Cal. "Honest I would."

"Loneliness is no fun, Chipmunk," he sighed, scratching around the electrodes on his chest. "And who knows how long we'll have the farm anyway?" He fixed his eyes on hers. "So how'd the story go? Kingsley like it enough to pay what it's worth?"

Rhonna paused, not sure whether or not to tell him the truth. But his light blue eyes under their sandy, irregular brows bored into hers, and she couldn't lie to him. "He had a choice between mine and a big league AP article on the conference. So I get zip. I wish I had better news."

He patted her hand and closed his eyes. "Well, we have another week before the tax sale. Anything can happen. The Lord will provide, your mother used to say, and she was just about always right."

His voice sounded tired, so Rhonna didn't say anything. Gradually his breathing became smooth and deep, broken only occasionally by shudders, as if suddenly his air supply was failing him. It was better to let him sleep, she thought. Time enough to talk about what had happened on Malta. When the nurse came in to tell her that visiting time was over, Rhonna left with relief, glad she had had no chance to tell him about Cal. Her father would know exactly what had happened. He would have looked into her eyes and felt as bad as she did. *He has enough pain of his own right now,* she thought. *Best I should keep mine to myself.*

"You should sell the farm fast," said Megan over dinner. "If the county assessor sells it for taxes, he'll let it go for anything he's offered. All they care about is covering the tax delinquency."

"The only ones who'd buy would be developers," said Rhonna hopelessly. "And I won't sell to someone who'd tear the place up."

"I'd buy it in a minute, if I had any money," Megan said. "How many old farmhouses are left on Long Island anymore? I know just what I'd do to turn that house into a decorator's dream."

It was true about Megan not having any money. The trust fund interest she got from her wealthy father and the small *Newstar* salary disappeared instantly into the flowing, magnificent dresses that masked Megan's weight problem and into redecorating her condo in downtown Southampton. She lived in style, but hardly had enough left for food, which she said, making a wry face, was just as well.

What Megan had said set Rhonna to thinking, and the next day, before visiting her father, she stopped at a real estate office. She talked to a brisk, efficient young woman, who knew exactly which property Rhonna was talking about. It seemed like everyone knew that little stretch of unspoiled beach and wanted the fun of spoiling it themselves.

"The house is worth nothing," the agent said. "A tear-down. Anyone who could afford that land could afford to put up a Tuscan-style villa."

Rhonna felt anger rip through her at hearing the house where she had grown up and been so happy called a tear-down. But she held her temper. "Then how about selling off a few acres?" she said.

The agent shook her head. "No good. I know that parcel. It's got only a seventy foot frontage on Dune Lane, even though it spreads out as you go in toward the ocean. The estates on both sides would never give you an easement."

That was true. Her father had tried, some years ago, to bring in a road that would allow him to build another house on the property. He had wanted to build one for Rhonna and a possible husband, but the house turned out to be as much a fantasy as the husband. Their neighbors, wealthy Manhattanites, refused the easement, saying he probably had in mind to build another rats' nest which would degrade their property values.

"Okay," Rhonna said, swallowing her rising desperation. "How about letting me run a long driveway into the beach area? I could sell the rest and put up a little place there, eventually."

"You'd have zoning problems. Everyone on that road would howl up a storm. No," the agent said, fiddling with the edges of what Rhonna could see was a listing form. "You'd be better off just to sell the whole thing. No one would want it without the beach frontage. I can take it off your hands fast, and you can pay the taxes out of your profit. And I have a nice little condo you could buy in Bridgehampton with what you'd have left after paying off the mortgage. What do you say?" The agent shoved the listing form at her, with a bright, brittle smile. Rhonna's words choked in her throat. She tied the fluttering ends of her blue scarf tightly around her neck and bolted out of the office. The next place she tried, the bank where she and her father had always done business, was just as unhelpful. The loan officer looked over the papers she brought and said the house was already mortgaged within an inch of its gabled roof. It was true, Rhonna realized, remembering how the taxes had been paid the year before last, when the potato crop failed during the heavy rains. God had provided, yes, but minimally. Now they were back in the hole again.

Who do I know that's really rich? Rich enough to give me an unsecured ten thousand dollar loan? For the first time, Rhonna wished she had cultivated some of the wealthy summer people whom she and her friends had always looked down on. The others, the year-round residents she'd grown up with, were all as poor as the Morans, unless they had sold their land and moved away.

There was nothing else to do but see if Ned Peavey would offer a loan on the place. He wouldn't demand his usual sleazy payment right away, if the episode with Cal's sister was any guide to his behavior. *By then,* she thought, *I'll have earned the money to pay him back. Kingsley will like my story enough to offer me the next plum that comes along at Newstar. I'm sure sure he will. Pretty sure, anyway.*

If it really was God's will for her to lose the farm, she would have to pray for the strength to accept the loss, but until then, she would keep fighting. In the old days, she would have lacked the confidence to fight, but something had happened to her since meeting Cal. It seemed like standing up to his toughness had made her stronger than she had ever been.

Rhonna pulled out Ned's card from her wallet and called him from the hospital, leaving a message that he should get in touch with her at the hospital or at home. She had a deal for him, was what she said, hoping he would read the wrong message into her words. It was the only way she could be sure he would call back.

Her father was sitting up in bed beaming at her. The IV was still in his arm, but the electrodes were gone and so were the nose tubes. He held out his arms.

"Good news, Chipmunk!" he cried. "I just had a visitor who wanted to buy the place."

"Dad, you didn't sell it!" Rhonna sank down on the chair beside his bed, wishing that the nose tubes were still there. She felt as if she could use a little extra oxygen.

"Not exactly. But I made a deal. " Moran rubbed his hands together. "I can live in the main house for the rest of my life. Then it goes to my buyer. Says he wants it for the woman he's going to marry. But get this, Rhonna. I got him to agree to build a place for you next to the beach, in your favorite spot. You have a lifetime lease on it, free. So you never have to leave the land."

"Dad, you should have asked me," Rhonna cried out so sharply that the nurse frowned in at the door.

"No time," Moran answered. "Mr. Conway was in a hurry. Had to leave for an assignment in Paris. The guy's some kind of reporter. Wonder how writing got him rich enough to put down six hundred thousand dollars."

"Cal Conway?" Rhonna's eyes opened wide. *The scoundrel,* she said to herself, *the selfish, rotten scoundrel.* He was buying it for Cristina and expected Rhonna to stay on the same property. Maybe even be his woman on the side. Convenient arrangement. She would be expected to keep an eye on the property while he and the contessa were jet-setting. "You mean Cal was here just now?"

"You know him?" Moran scratched his head. "I seem to be missing a piece. Did you tell me about Cal Conway?"

"I was going to." Rhonna put her face in her hands, not wanting her father to see the expression on it. "We met on Malta. I hate to say how close we got, or almost got."

"Can't blame you for that," Moran said, reaching out to pull her hands away from her face. "He's a nice guy. Close- mouthed, though. I couldn't get much out of him about his plans for the place."

"Why am I not surprised at that?" Rhonna got up and paced around the bed. "He's planning to marry an Italian countess whose father is an ambassador or something. Maybe turn the house into a hotel. They'll fit right into Southampton high society."

Moran's face wrinkled in concern. "But I thought you said he was after you, Chipmunk."

"For people like us, that would be a problem," Rhonna said, folding her arms tightly over her chest and staring out the window into the parking lot. "Not for him. He's got the morals of a feral cat."

"I thought he seemed pretty honest," Moran sighed. "He had me fooled."

"Me too." Rhonna felt her voice shake and stopped talking for a moment while she got control of herself. "Look, Dad, I happen to know that even though you've signed the papers, you legally have five days to change your mind. We can find another way."

"We're at the end of the line with the farm," Moran said sadly. "You know that."

"If I can get another deal, a better one," Rhonna said, leaning over her father and putting her hands on his shoulders, "will you break the contract with Conway?"

"Sure. You go ahead and try. I don't want to see you eating your heart out over this guy and him living right next door." Moran patted her cheek gently. "Now, I gotta lie down, Chipmunk. My head feels too heavy to hold up any more."

"I shouldn't have talked to you about this," Rhonna worried, adjusting his pillow and cranking down the bed. "It's the last thing you need."

"Of course we should talk," Moran said. "About anything. You go do what you can, Rhonna. I'll sit on the deal for as long as we've got."

Rhonna kissed her father on the forehead and dashed for home, hoping to catch Ned's phone call, if there was going to be one. A yellow taxi was waiting on Dune Lane, by the Moran's mail box when she drove up. Rhonna narrowed her eyes, trying to see into the bright sunshine and determine who was waiting for her. As she pulled into the long driveway, the wheels crunching on the stones, she looked back through the rear view mirror and almost ran into a maple tree beside the driveway when she saw who was coming toward her from the cab. She slammed on the brake and jumped out of the truck, leaving the motor running and the door hanging open.

"Cal Conway, you get off my property," she cried, her voice breaking. She wiped the heels of her palms into her eyes to get rid of a sudden rush of tears. "You've got the chutzpah to face me after what you've done?" She stood still, her hands on both hips, refusing to come closer.

Cal walked toward her, ignoring her order. He looked pale and tired, as if he'd been travelling non-stop for too long. "I did what I had to do, Rhonna."

"You had to buy my house for you and Cristina?" A wild, bitter laugh rose in Rhonna's throat and almost choked her. "Just because she wanted it? Come on, Cal. I know you better than that."

Cal took a few long strides and was beside her. "I asked you to trust me, Rhonna. There's a lot I can't tell you right now." "Trust!" Rhonna turned on her heel and started back to the truck. "Man, after what you've done to me, I wouldn't trust you to tie my shoes. You'd probably knot them together, and I'd fall on my face. Bumping my story at *Newstar* really did me in. You knew it would."

"Bumping your story... Cal shook his head. "But that wasn't me..."

"Don't act so innocent," Rhonna stormed. "I saw your AP story rolling off the fax machine with my own eyes."

"Rhonna, that's all done by AP," he said, sounding so honest that she almost believed him. "I wouldn't have done that to you. To you of all people. You can't believe that."

"You bet I can." Rhonna stood back a few steps, so get away from the warm, intense aura that swept her toward him. "You knew if I couldn't sell that story and pay my taxes, I'd lose the place. Who else knew that?"

"I wouldn't have sabotaged you, Rhonna," Cal said steadily, his eyes holding hers. "At worst, you'd have the beach land and your own place. Your father seemed to think that would be okay with you."

"Don't you talk about my father. That innocent, gentle man," Rhonna whispered, feeling her voice die in her throat. "You aren't fit to be in the same room with him."

The taxi driver honked, and Cal stepped away from her. "Look," he said fiercely, "I can't explain any of this. Not now. My plane was delayed only an hour and that's why I could get here at all. I'm on my way to Paris. Will you come with me?"

"Don't even think about it." Rhonna pulled away from him. "I've got to stay with my father and see what I can do to stop him selling our place to you. Just thought you ought to know that."

"Don't, sweetheart," Cal said over his shoulder as he ran for the taxi. "Don't do anything until I get back next week. Trust me that much. You can find my lawyer, Sean Feeney, downtown. Call him if you need anything."

Rhonna watched as Cal bent to get in the car, his lithe, lean body looking taut as a bow, his face grim, already reflecting whatever it was he was going to do next, his mind already off her. He was probably meeting Cristina in Paris, she told herself, getting back into the truck and grinding the gears as she drove down to the garage. *As for his lawyer,* Rhonna thought, *I'd rot like a dead seal on the beach before I'd ask for anything from him.* If Cal knew her at all, he would have known that.

"I wouldn't trust you as far as I could throw a sack of potatoes," she muttered. But in her heart she felt a sad hollowness that made her want to cry. Her desire for Cal was pushing God out of her heart, Rhonna felt, leaving her in turmoil. *What kind of life would it be,* she wondered, *what if there was no closeness to God that would give me peace when Cal turns my life upside down?* She went upstairs into her bedroom and threw herself face down on her familiar flowered quilt, sobbing until she had no tears left.

Just as she was starting to fall asleep, totally cried out, Rhonna heard the phone ring in the first floor hall. At first she lay there, not caring, but then she figured it could be Ned, her last hope. She went downstairs and picked up the phone, feeling the urge to wrap something around it, so the voice on the other end wouldn't contaminate her hands.

"Hey, gorgeous one," came Ned's voice, sliding around the words, "I hear you want me."

"I want a loan," Rhonna said coolly, wishing she could sound that way when she talked to Cal Conway. "Twenty thousand. A second mortgage on my property here in Southampton, as security. Can you do that?"

"Not only can, but will." Ned sounded like he was smiling, stretching his vowels with his thick lips. "See you at the Water Mill Inn for lunch tomorrow?"

"Where are you?" Rhonna had thought he was on his way to Washington.

"Manhattan. I had an idea you might be calling." Ned was slow-voiced, as if his mouth were full of honey. "Twelve noon?"

"Okay. Water Mill Inn it is. Bring your worldly goods."

Rhonna hung up, feeling like she was about to be sick. How much better was she than Cristina Montani, she thought, as she sat down in the beat-up little church pew some ancestor had put in the hall, never dreaming it would someday be a telephone seat. Like Cristina, she was playing Ned for all he was worth, just as he played women. If Cal hadn't gotten her into this spot, Rhonna said aloud, suppressing another rush of tears, she would be a free person, as she had been when only God and her father mattered. She would be able to pay her debts, own her home again, keep her father from giving up and dying with another heart attack. And Cal? He was flying back to Paris and Cristina. What did he care how miserable she was? She had always felt loyalty was not the strong suit of jet-setters, and now she was sure.

Rhonna went slowly upstairs, undressing as she went, glad to get the fancy clothes off and be herself again. She tossed her suit and lacy slip on the bed and pulled on her shorts and sweatshirt. There was still the beach, she said to herself, still her secret place where Cal had never been and couldn't reach her.

She climbed down the rocks at the end of the dirt road, sliding part of the way because rain had washed out a section of her usual climbing path. When she faced the ocean, seeing its slow, gentle waves scallop the sand, Rhonna breathed deeply, feeling like she was home at last. High rocks curved around her fifty feet of beach like embracing arms, keeping it completely private except at the lowest of tides. It looked to her a little like the beach below the temple on Malta, and Rhonna ran through her memory of the scenes there. Cal watching her dance, Cal kissing her breathless, Cal climbing down the rocks to save the kids in the sailboat. They had shared so much in their short week together, Rhonna whispered to herself, sitting against her favorite rock and putting her face up to catch the sun. Now he was running off to someone else, having taken everything from her. *Leaving me with nothing, not even a heart in one piece.*

"No," she shouted aloud, waving her fist in the air and dancing a few steps, like a fighter in the ring. "You haven't got me down yet, Cal Conway."

She was glad that she had not given in to him, or she would be irretrievably lost now. He had not, after all, taken everything. To have lost him after giving herself entirely would have buried her in shame. As it was, she was about up to her chin in it, and fighting hard to keep what she had left of her pride. He didn't deserve to know she loved him, not unless he loved her too and said so. Fair was fair. The man had altogether too much pride for his own good and certainly for hers.

Rhonna bent over, straight-legged, to touch her toes, then stood tall and stretched her arms to the sky. *I'm well rid of a man who thinks he can mop the floor with me,* she said to herself, *and then keep me in a nearby house to serve any use he might make of me. Girlfriend, gatekeeper, housekeeper, baby-sitter. . .* Rhonna began to run up and down the beach flailing her arms to use maximum energy. The thought of Cal and Cristina having babies, walking them on this beach where she herself had played as a child made Rhonna sick to her stomach. She stopped running, held her arms tightly over her midsection and gasped for air. How could he think she would stay in her little beachhouse to watch him enjoy family life with another woman? Rhonna clenched her fists. *I would do anything to stop him from taking my home away from me,* she told herself. *Well, anything that wasn't illegal or immoral.*

"Hold that thought," she said aloud as she climbed up the rocky rise, back to the road. "Don't let the fact that Dad likes him or that you love him stand in the way. Cal trades on his charm, that's clear. With me, it's not going to work."

She stood for a moment and looked back at the water, framed by the scrub oak trees that curved to touch each other at the top like old friends meeting. How she would have loved to show this to Cal, she thought, her throat aching with the pressure of unshed tears. Loved to swim with him, lie on the beach all day with him and feel their skin touching from head to toe, their hands running over each other, discovering every beloved part, turning each other to molten fire as they had in that Malta hotel room. Rhonna felt her body shake inside, as if Cal's hands were still on her, and she closed her eyes. It was no use lying to herself. She still wanted him so much she could almost smell the crisp, piney aroma of the man. Even here, in her most cherished, private place, he invaded her senses, caught her heart in his hands and wouldn't let go.

Rhonna ran all the way back to the house, wishing she could leave him behind. She willed herself to think only of her father and managed to do just that for the length of time it took her to shower, dress, and turn the truck around. Then she stopped, the tires skidding on the stones. Right here was where he had been this afternoon. Right here he had crushed her in his arms, whispered kisses on her eyes, her cheeks, her lips. He was a man who would take years, maybe a lifetime, to get over, Rhonna said to herself, gunning her engine fiercely. She had better start right now, if she meant business.

Chapter Seven

Since she was driving her old truck and wearing her five-year-old yellow cotton sundress, Rhonna was not surprised when the waiter blocked her way at the door. Only when she said she was with Ned Peavey did he smile and lead her over to a window table that overlooked the stream and old mill. Ned rose to meet her and took both her hands in his big, beefy ones.

"I figured we'd meet again," he said eagerly, "Here, sit down. I've ordered us two dry martinis." He reluctantly let go of her so she could sit down, but not without giving her fingers a hard, damp, meaningful squeeze.

Rhonna put her hands in her lap as soon as they were released. She tried to smile, but the edges of her lips trembled and didn't cooperate. "I wonder if you're so keen on seeing me just because Cal and I were involved," she said. "Is that possible?" She didn't care very much, but could think of nothing else to say to this pushy, unappetizing man.

"Doesn't hurt," Ned grinned his gap-toothed grin at her. "As I said, I owe him one."

"You said that, yes." Rhonna pretended to taste her drink, then pushed it away. She needed a clear head and had no intention of letting Ned take charge. She had a sudden idea. *The man's an egotist. Well, then, use his ego.* "I've been thinking of doing a story on you," she said, with an effort at a smile. "I'm a journalist."

The waiter hovered behind Ned, bowing and smiling.

"I know. Don't think I haven't had you checked out." Ned pointed to items on the menu and ordered for her without asking her what she wanted. "What kind of story?"

"Oh, you know," Rhonna said, waving her hand, purposefully vague. "On your life, your accomplishments, your plans. I think people would like to know."

"I bet they would," Ned laughed with a snort, and tossed down another gulp of his martini. "First, let's talk about the property. The loan. You wanted twenty thousand?" He pulled a checkbook out of one pocket and a legal document out of another. "Look this over and tell your father to sign here." He indicated a checked signature line.

"Just like that?" Rhonna felt her brow wrinkle. "Don't you want to know anything about the place or why I want the loan?"

"I make it my business to know before I come to a meeting," Ned said, attacking the shrimp louis the waiter brought him. "I know about the foreclosure coming up, and I know Cal Conway is trying to buy the place."

"Did he tell you that?" Rhonna's head was swimming. She felt as if she were in free fall. Her salmon croquettes sat untouched in front of her.

"He didn't need to. I have my informants." Ned gestured with his fork and Rhonna moved instinctively away, as if she was about to be impaled. "Reliable informed sources, they call it in your trade, right?" He smiled, putting his head to one side, apparently wanting to appear charming. "Here, just try the croquettes."

He stabbed one with his fork and held it to her lips. Reluctantly she took the bite. "Very nice," she muttered, hardly able to swallow. "Thank you, but I can feed myself." She picked up the document and read through it, fighting the cloudy legal language.

Rhonna remembered the conversation she had overheard between Ned and Cristina at the Malta ball. "How do I know this isn't the resort land you and Cristina would like to buy up?"

Ned's irregular eyebrows drew tightly together. "How the devil did you know about that?"

"Let's just say you can't trust Cristina with your business," Rhonna said lightly. "I need to know you aren't trying to buy up my land and turn it into a playground for the jet set." "Show your lawyer," Ned advised. "He'll tell you a second mortgage is worth squat. I'm just doing you a favor, baby. Believe it."

"It says here that if in one month I don't come up with the twenty thousand you take my dad's place on the title to the property." Rhonna read off the passage that had grabbed her attention. "That doesn't give me much time."

"Take it or leave it," Ned said wolfing down the last shreds of his shrimp. "Anyone you ask will tell you I drive a hard bargain. I told you a second mortgage is nothing to worry about."

That was true, Rhonna thought. The bank held the first mortgage, and if there was any foreclosure, the bank would get its money back before Ned got his. A hard little voice spoke in the back of her mind, saying that she would rather the bank get the property than for Cal and Cristina to have it.

"Besides Ned added, slugging down the rest of his martini, "if I'm on title you'll be protected. I'll make sure of that, since we're friends now. Right, sweetie?"

"I'm not sure," she said finally, putting the document in her purse. "I'll run it by our lawyer. If he says it's okay, I'll give it to my dad tonight."

"Good," Ned said, picking up her martini glass and draining it. "I'll meet you at the hospital at four this afternoon. Your dad's room. We'll talk about that article afterward, over dinner."

She felt a shiver of reluctance when she thought of introducing this man to her father, but it was reasonable for Ned to expect the meeting. After all, her father was the one getting the loan, not her.

When she had agreed, Ned took her arm and steered her out the door. "I have a nice room upstairs," he said, his smile turning wolfish. "Pretty view. It would look prettier with you in it."

"The farm is your collateral," Rhonna said steadily, pulling away from the ham-like hand clutching her arm. "Not me."

Ned let her go, with a forced laugh. "Okay, sweetie. I get you. Now's not the time. Tomorrow, then."

She walked away, looking for a valet to retrieve her truck from whatever mysterious place they had hidden it. The sound of his words rang unpleasantly in her ears. 'I get you,' he had said ambivalently.

"In your dreams, dude," she muttered.

As she tipped the valet and drove away, Rhonna was already compiling a list of questions she meant to ask Ned Peavey during their interview. *Maybe this story will be the one that will make me enough money to pay him off. A month isn't much to work with,* Rhonna thought nervously, *but I have to play the cards I've been dealt.* Maybe Ned Peavey, in his own awful way, was the answer to prayer that she'd been asking for. *God works mysteriously, and maybe,* she thought, *this is a case in point.*

"The lawyer says it's okay," Rhonna said, leaning over her father's shoulder as he read the document.

"If I sign this," Moran said, closing his eyes and leaning back against the pillow, "we might get zero from the sale, if there has to be one."

"We've got a month, Dad," she urged. "Anything can happen."

"What about Cal Conway?"

"What about him? I'll go to that lawyer of his today and tell him the deal's off. We've got the right to change our minds. All you have to do is sign this paper. Our lawyer said it makes the sale to Cal null and void."

"If that's what you want." Moran sighed and wrote his name on both documents. "I won't be around that much longer, Chipmunk. You'd better take charge from now on."

"Don't say that, Dad." Rhonna hugged him fiercely. "Once this trouble is off your back, you'll be fine."

"Knock, knock," Ned walked in the door and sat down by Moran's bed, and stuck out his hand "I'm your lender, Ned Peavey. A friend of your daughter's." He grinned at Rhonna.

"Al Moran." Her father returned the handshake, but pulled his hand away quickly. "I've signed the document."

"If you don't mind," Ned said as a nurse came in, "I'd like you to sign it again and have this charming young lady witness the signature. You don't mind, do you?"

Moran agreed, and Ned tucked the document into the inside pocket of his pin-striped blazer. Then he turned to Rhonna. "See you at the Inn tonight for dinner at six?"

"Okay if I bring a tape recorder?" Rhonna half-turned in her chair, but did not get up.

"Not okay. And don't try to stash one someplace. I've been known to personally frisk my female interviewers." Ned gave her a wink as he left.

"I don't like that man, Chipmunk," Moran said, tugging at his pillow as if it was fighting him. "Cal Conway was a lot more like it."

"Why?" Rhonna leaned over and took his hand, then held it tightly. "Tell me what you liked about Cal."

"He was straightforward. Like you." Moran stroked her fingers and stared into space. "Didn't run his mouth a lot."

"He's got plenty to hide, that's why," Rhonna said. She paused, then asked haltingly, "Did he ask about me?"

"Matter of fact, yes. He wondered what you were like as a little girl." Moran grinned at her affectionately and rumpled her hair. "My favorite subject. I told him how you used to get your letters printed in the local paper when you were on a tear about people killing whales, and how you won a 4H blue ribbon for raising that foal you were so crazy about. He wouldn't let me stop talking."

"I hope you didn't tell him how I was voted the graduate most likely to make trouble," Rhonna said, shaking her head. Cal had quite enough on her already, while she knew next to nothing about him.

"Sure. And about how I got to calling you Chipmunk. He got a good laugh out of that." Moran looked at her suddenly. "You know, I just don't get it. Why don't you like this guy? I'd have sworn you two were made for each other."

Rhonna pulled her hand away from his and stood up. "Dad, you don't know how ruthless he is. I didn't either, at first. He sold out his own family." She didn't say Cal had done it to expose some shady dealings by the same Ned Peavey who had just taken over their mortgage.

"He'd do anything to get a story before someone else can. He got my article on Malta bumped from *Newstar*, if you want to know. I'll never forgive him for that. And he knew why I needed the money too." Rhonna clenched her fists. "I wouldn't believe a word he said if he swore on his family Bible."

"Well, I wouldn't have thought bad of him," Moran said, pulling his covers up to his chin and closing his eyes. "He seemed like the kind I'd always hoped you'd wind up with, Chipmunk. Appreciates you, he does."

Rhonna leaned over and kissed her father's forehead. "Dad, I wish your liking him could change what he is. Sleep now. I'll be back later." She decided not to say that she'd fallen in love with Cal. Her father would only feel worse, and he felt bad enough already.

After he had closed his eyes, she stood by the door for a few minutes, praying for this good, simple man who had served God and family all his life. *Dear Lord Jesus, don't let him lose the farm and die in a stranger's bed.* She wiped her eyes with the backs of her hands. *But whatever happens, help me accept your will.* Her next stop was at Sean Feeney's office, an understated, elegantly paneled suite over Southampton's most exclusive men's shop. As she passed the display window, Rhonna looked in, thinking Cal must get his imported wool sweaters there. She paused for a moment, gazing at a maroon tweed from Scotland. How she would have loved touching that sweater if it were over Cal's broad chest, and seeing the way it picked up the ruddy hue of his auburn hair. *What if I just went in and bought it for him? Gave it to him when he comes back? Made peace with him? He would think me a fool, that's what.* He was taking everything she loved away from her, and here she was thinking what more she could give him. *Dummy*, Rhonna said angrily to herself. *Idiot. When will you* learn?

Sean Feeney showed her in immediately. He was a tall man with narrow shoulders, rounded at the belly with middle age, and sporting a thick, curly gray beard that compensated for the total lack of hair on his head. His smile was gentle, and Rhonna felt unexplainably at ease, given that this was the man representing Cal in the snatching of her property. Not wanting to be further manipulated, Rhonna made her voice harsh.

"Mr. Feeney, Cal Conway said I should contact you. Here's the paper that releases us from the deal. I have a loan."

Feeney looked at the paper, then frowned, his face looking as crumpled as though she had punched it. "And the lender wouldn't be Ned Peavey, now, would it?"

"That's exactly who. You can tell Cal Conway that he won't get my home that easily."

"Ah, my dear," Feeney said, his gray brows closing over his long nose, "You're playing footsie with the devil, y'know. Ned Peavey's not a good man. No, he is not.' Feeney shook his bald head slowly and sorrowfully.

"He was good enough to take a second mortgage on my place, so I don't have to sell it." Rhonna found it hard to breathe, and put her hand to her throat.

"Hush, hush, my girl," Feeney said softly. "Let's just make a call to the bank."

Rhonna plumped herself down in a vacant leather chair and waited while Feeney talked.

He hung up and scratched his beard as if it were inhabited. "It's as I thought, Miss Moran. This morning Ned Peavey bought the first mortgage to your property, along with a few others. As I said, he is not a man to be trusted."

Rhonna put her palms over her eyes and dug in, to stop the tears. She whispered to herself the few bad words she knew. So, Ned had known all the time how to get hold of 99 Dune Road.

She ought to have been aware of that, having overheard his conversation with Cristina about making a hotel on prime oceanfront Southampton property. But his holding a second mortgage had seemed so harmless. And Cal's buying the place for Cristina had seemed so intolerable. Rhonna's breath caught raggedly in her throat. *Oh dear God, what have I done?*

"I had no idea Ned held the first mortgage," she choked out when she could finally speak. "Can I get out of this contract?"

Feeney helped her up and walked with her to the door. His prominent, sensitive brown eyes were as sad as hers. "No. You've got yourself in a box, Miss Moran. I wish I knew how to help you."

A box it was, Rhonna said, driving too fast all the way home. Whichever way she jumped, either Cal or Ned had her trapped. She sped along the narrow street that turned into Dune Road, barely avoiding a taxi that was pulling out of the new mall that blotched the landscape. She had known she couldn't trust either Cal or Ned, but hadn't realized which one was more dangerous.

As she turned into the driveway, Rhonna spotted a taxi parked by the mailbox. Her heart jumped, thinking it might be Cal. Maybe he'd had second thoughts. Maybe he'd decided to come back. She could taste his kisses on her lips and her knees weakened at the imaginary touch of his strong hands. She parked the truck and jumped out, wiping her damp palms on her jacket.

Out of the taxi walked Cristina Montani, her black curls flawlessly arranged around her shoulders, set off by a red silk top with thin straps. Her tight black pants rippled over her aerobically trim legs.

"You do not mind if I take a very small look?" Cristina said with a toothy, expensive looking smile. "After all, it will be my home."

"Not real soon, it won't," Rhonna said, shoving her hands in the pockets of her jeans. "I wouldn't start counting the pine trees, if I were you."

"I count everything, my dear," Cristina purred. "Something you should learn to do."

"You think Cal's got this place sewed up for you and him?" Rhonna placed her feet firmly on the gravel. "Forget it."

Cristina tossed a gleaming tress over one shoulder, smiling confidently. "You think Cal bought this place for me?"

"I think he tried to." Rhonna's voice was stronger than she expected it to be.

Cristina shrugged. "One way or another, it will be mine," she said. "And you will be leaving soon. I suggest you start packing." She swung her full hips lazily as she walked back to the waiting taxi, then half turned for a moment. "Though you probably have nothing much to pack." She looked Rhonna's old sundress up and down, rolled her eyes, and left.

"And she let me know I looked like Mrs. Potato-head," Rhonna stormed to Megan, putting her head down on the desk so her friend wouldn't see her tears. "Made me feel like a bug that crawled under the door to eat the wood." Megan loosened her belt a little so she could finish her take-out tuna melt. Then she leaned her elbows on the desk and stared at Rhonna. "You say she seemed surprised that Cal had tried to buy the place?"

"Well, yes. But he's away. Hasn't had time to tell Cristina anything."

Megan fluffed her bangs with her fingertips. "I invite you to consider who has had time to tell this wicked Witch of the West about the sale of your property."

Rhonna wiped her eyes and stared back at Megan. "You mean Ned? You think maybe Ned told her he was buying the place? Why would he do that? They're not even friends anymore."

"I don't know. You said those two were in cahoots on Malta. Maybe they decided to work together after all."

Rhonna shook her head. "They didn't sound like they were getting along. I could have sworn Ned was planning to bump her out of his business plans."

"Then you'll just have to find out from him. You said you had an interview with him tonight. So, go for it. I'm praying for you, honey, like you always have for me."

Bill Kingsley called Rhonna into his office. From the tense sound of his voice, she thought she'd better hurry. With a quick wave to Megan, Rhonna ran inside the office and shut the glass door behind her.

"What's up?" She sat on the tip of the wide, wooden swivel chair opposite Bill's.

"Remember that Malta story you brought back?" Bill pressed his fingertips tightly together.

"Too well," Rhonna replied, thinking how close she had come to tearing it up and giving the pieces to Cal.

"I faxed it last night to the editor at *Fortune,* a friend of mine for a lot of years." Bill was jubilant. "The guy just called me back. Thinks the editorial board will agree to take it. Brilliant job, he said. How'd you like that?"

Rhonna touched her tight throat, thinking it would never again loosen up so she could take a breath. "They pay pretty well, don't they?"

"Honey, the pay's the least of it." Bill leaned forward and grabbed her hands. "You got a future in this business, now. Yeah, they pay well. A thousand just for the kill fee."

"Kill fee?" Rhonna felt stupid, but she was new to this world of publishing.

"You know, the money they pay you if they can't use your story after all." Bill waved his hand carelessly. "But that's not going to happen. You'll get ten thousand for this one, easy."

"And more, if I can bring off an exclusive interview with Ned Peavey?"

"You do that, honey, and they'll probably push you for a Pulitzer Prize. Ned Peavey talks to nobody. You get him to talk to you, and you can name your ticket."

"He's talking to me tonight, at the Water Mill Inn," Rhonna said, feeling a little pride rising in her as Bill's eyes opened wide.

"Well, make the most of it. See if you can find out what his plans are for the Adirondack reserve." Bill wadded up a piece of paper and threw it with a flourish into the waste basket across the room.

"I got an anonymous tip today that the President's about to sign a bill to give the high mountain areas to Peavey Corp. for a few billion." Bill grimaced, and his cheaters slid further down his nose. "Just like the Dutchman that bought Manhattan from that Indian for twenty-four bucks. Check it out."

"I heard Ned say he had something like that in mind." Rhonna slung the strap of her purse over her shoulder and was already at the door.

Bill's eyes opened wide again. "Good work, honey. But watch it. This Peavey guy doesn't play nice. When he says he wants to have you for dinner, that's exactly what he means."

Bill Kingsley was right, Rhonna thought, as she got herself into her new black jersey dress and wrapped Megan's Moroccan shawl around her shoulders. She would have to use every strategy to get around Ned Peavey. In the folds of the heavy, woven shawl, she had sewn an inside pocket and tucked Megan's tiny tape recorder into it. Her friend used it to record her diet advisor's expensive classes, as clandestine an operation as the one Rhonna herself was about to engage in. *Good thing Megan's praying for me,* Rhonna thought, *since my head's too rattled to pray for anything but dad's life.*

Ned rose as Rhonna came to the table and watched appreciatively as she arranged the scarf carefully across the back of the chair, not exposing the pocket. His eyes roved up and down the short, form-fitting halter dress.

"Guess I don't need to frisk you, gorgeous one," he said. "Though I'd sure like to. I'll need to look in your purse though, okay?"

Rhonna nodded, pushing the small black patent leather bag across the table. "Go ahead."

Ned explored her few belongings with his beefy forefinger, and Rhonna said to herself, *I'd like to throw away everything he's touched.*

He looked up and smiled. "You travel light," he remarked.

"My notebook and pen are all I need." Rhonna put the small notebook on table and snapped her pen open. "And you to be up front. I'll need that too. Tell me about your family. Did your father make the Peavey fortune, or did you?"

Ned ordered a seafood paella and a liter of Bordeaux wine. Before his food arrived, he demolished the bowl of macadamia nuts and snapped his fingers for more. "My father was a miner in the New York State mountains," he said. "Never amounted to much. Liked to fool around in Adirondack caves. He got queasy in one of them. Crawled down to the highway real sick, and covered with splotches. Then he died." Peavey grinned. "You've heard that saying, 'Life's hard, and then you die?' Well, my father could have written that. Old goat never provided anything much for me. Lucky I had the stuff to make it on my own."

Rhonna's pen stopped for a moment. Could old Mr. Peavey have stumbled onto some radioactive material in one of those caves? She would have to ask carefully. "Did he leave you any maps or anything that you could use later? I mean something that might tell you which forests were best for cutting?"

"Matter of fact, yes." Ned was already working his way through the liter of wine. "Those maps are a treasure. My father was an artist, in his way. How'd you like to see them?"

Rhonna was instantly on her guard. "I assume they're not in a museum?"

"In my Manhattan penthouse, right on the wall," he said, licking the wine off his thick lips. "You're invited anytime."

"I'd have to give that some thought," Rhonna said, taking a small bite of her paella. "Right now I'd like to know how you plan to get the president to sign that new bill. You know, the one that would let selected areas of national parks go into private hands?"

Ned frowned and put down his fork. "You know about that? Well, of course you do. You've been hanging with Cal Conway." He smiled an artificially sweet smile. "Let's just say a lot of corporations, including mine, are more concerned to makes lot of American jobs than about the fate of a few owls and mud lizards. And you can quote me on that."

"You think that the new idea of protecting whole ecosystems might work better than protecting a few species?" Rhonna hoped to catch him in a contradiction.

"Honey, I think we'd be better off protecting businessmen like me who would rather give jobs to American workers than save spotted owls. And you can quote me on that too."

"I'll do that." Rhonna decided to risk being offensive. "What happens to the logging and milling jobs when the prime forest growth is gone?"

"You think that's all we're after in those mountains?" Ned drained the last of the wine, tossing it down like the Perrier water Rhonna was drinking.

"I don't know. Is it? You said something on the plane about minerals up there." She was pushing too hard, but hoped Ned's drinks would work to her advantage as they had before.

"Did I?" Ned's smiled turned down at the corners, giving his face a cruel cast. "Don't quote me on that. I'll make you look bad if you do. And a girl as pretty as you wants to keep on looking good, right?" He leaned across the table and snatched up her notebook.

Rhonna let him look through it, since nothing was there that could incriminate her in his eyes. His jovial tone didn't fool her, nor did his veiled threats come as a surprise. He was a dangerous man, but at least what you saw was what you got. In Cal's case, what you saw drove you crazy with longing, and what you got was nothing. Ned, bad as he was, at least had potential. He might wind up as one story Cal wouldn't get.

"Looks like you'll give me a good press." Ned closed the notebook and gave it back to her. "I'll expect to read your story before it comes out. How about bringing it to New York when you've got a draft ready? We'll take in a Broadway show, and I'll let you see those maps."

"Only if you'll bring them down to the lobby," Rhonna said cautiously. "And if you'll tell me what Cristina Montani is doing in your life."

"I don't talk about my women to each other. It's probably the only sin I haven't committed in my checkered career. Ask her, if you want to know." Ned waved his hand expansively. "Now, tell me what you'd like to know about Peavey Corporation's rise from zilch to zillions. About that, I got no trouble talking."

Rhonna didn't escape till midnight from Peavey's self-promotional corporate history, glad that the important words had been spoken early in the evening and were captured on the tape recorder. She left Ned at their table, nodding over a Grand Marnier, and fled home.

The house felt empty without her father there to greet her, as he always had, with hot chocolate and questions about the evening. She never had to hide anything from him, for he would not have withheld love, whatever she had done. Not that she had ever done anything to be ashamed of before her father or God.

"It's your life," was Ed Moran's favorite comment. No wonder she'd never, until Cal, found a man she wanted to give herself to. Al Moran was tall competition. Too bad Cal didn't have her father's integrity and unconditional love. It was enough that her body was playing mysterious games with her. She didn't need a man who could strum her like a guitar.

She lay down finally, after pacing around the big, empty house, and her body ached as she remembered how Cal's lips and hands had brought it alive. Unable to sleep, she pulled her big white teddy bear, a tenth-birthday gift from her father, into her arms and hugged it fiercely. It was usually enough, but not now, not since Cal had held her close back on Malta, and she had felt his body flame against hers. Not since she had felt his lips breathe his warmth into her. *Nothing, no one, will ever be enough for me again.* Rhonna flung the teddy bear off the bed, put her head under the pillow, and closed her eyes tightly so the tears wouldn't roll out. She felt so heavily armored that she couldn't even pray. How could she, when what she really wanted God to give her was the very man He could not want for her? *Lord, help me, I so want to be his and Yours too. Please, please find a way.*

Bill Kingsley called early, waking Rhonna out of a sound, exhausted sleep, telling her he had some good news. She should come right over to the office, he told her, before going to the hospital. Rhonna tied her hair in a pony tail, put on her favorite denim jumpsuit, and drove downtown so fast that she would have gotten a ticket, if the cop who pulled her over hadn't been an old admirer from high school days.

"Any word from *Fortune*?" She had to sit down in order to get her breath.

Bill gave her cold water in a paper cup. "The editorial board agreed. They'll definitely take the article," he said. "I told them you had a pipeline to Ned Peavey, and they want anything on him you can get. The in with Peavey cinched the sale."

"How much?" Rhonna took a deep breath. "When?"

"Ten thousand, in two months, when the article's printed." Bill sat back in his chair, smiling around his celebratory cigar. "It's for the article and the Peavey interview as well."

"Two months!" Rhonna's shoulders sagged. "I've got to have that money now. Can't they give me an advance?"

"I asked, as a personal favor," Bill said. "But two thousand was all I could get upfront."

Rhonna clenched her hands and pounded her fists against her knees. "If I could just get Ned Peavey to wait that extra month. But he wouldn't. Not that one. He's got his reasons for boxing me in."

"You might be interested in this message." Bill tossed the pink message pad across the desk. "For some reason, Cal Conway's mother's trying to get hold of you."

Rhonna was too stunned to pick the message up. Cal's mother had no reason to call her. How could she even know Rhonna existed? Given how rarely Cal contacted his mother, she could hardly be sure *he* existed.

"Did you talk to her?" Rhonna held her small, tense hands tightly together, trying to stay calm. "Did she tell you what she wanted?"

"Sounded to me like a real nice lady who wants her son back." Bill tapped the long ash of his cigar on the edge of the empty coffee can that served him as an ashtray.

"We talked for a few minutes, but she said you're the one she needs to talk to. Stay here and call her. I've got to go talk to the people over in Classified about their lousy proofreading. They've got an ad that says they're selling a wife- sized stuffed baby elephant. I think they mean 'life-sized,' but with these guys, you never know."

Rhonna waited a few minutes after she was alone, opening her cell phone, then closing it. She bit the tip off one of her nails before she could finally dial. What could this woman want from her? Cal had said his parents were rich and hopelessly out of touch with the needs of ordinary people like herself. She dialed the number on the message pad and tapped her fingernails hard on Bill Kingsley's cluttered desk while she waited for someone to pick up the phone.

"Conway residence," a cool male voice said, sounding the way Rhonna assumed a butler was likely to sound. Not that she'd ever called anyone with a butler before. "Whom do you wish to speak to?"

"I'm Rhonna Moran," she said, trying to keep her voice as cool as his. "Returning Mrs. Conway's call."

It took a few minutes for Cal's mother to be located. Having breakfast in bed, no doubt. Rhonna felt her heart hardening, not wanting to like these people. They had produced a man who caused her pain, and they had caused him pain too. Probably it had been his parents who had turned him so hard. She had no intention of being friendly.

"Miss Moran?" A gentle, tentative voice came over the wire. "I'm Ellen Conway, Cal's mother. I realize I'm a stranger. Would it be too much to ask you to meet me for lunch today at the Old Post Inn?"

"But...why...," Rhonna floundered, not sure how to deal with this sweet, disembodied voice. "I'd like some idea of what you have in mind," she finished, not knowing what else to say.

"You could be of help," Mrs. Conway said, sounding as shy as Rhonna felt. "I'd like to explain why in person."

Rhonna gave in, as she always did when people were being as sweet as Mrs. Conway was. The way to Rhonna's heart was to ask for help, though she tried not to let anyone know it. "Of course. I'll meet you at noon, after I visit my father in the hospital."

"Yes, Cal told me about that. I'll wait as long as you need me to, my dear." The soft, elegant voice faded as Mrs. Conway said good-by.

"You're going to have lunch with your beloved's rich snoot of a mother dressed like *that*?" Megan's shrilled at her. "You look like something out of a country western. Let's get right over to Lily

Paul's. She's got a mauve silk suit in the window that's begging you to get in it and walk away."

Rhonna looked down ruefully at her denim jumpsuit. "It's that bad?" She said doubtfully. "Megan, I can't afford anything at Lily Paul's."

"You just got a two thousand dollar advance on that article. It's all over the office. Come on, you can't afford to have Mrs. Conway think you're a Shinnecock hillbilly."

"I don't know." Rhonna calculated whether or not she had time to drive home before heading back for the hospital and lunch engagements. No way. "How much is this mauve thing?"

"It's on sale for just a hundred fifty. And there's a little ivory surplice blouse with it for fifty more. Come on. I'll buy you the blouse for a Christmas present. And let's turn that pony tail into a French twist, okay?"

"I can't let you buy me any more clothes, Megan," Rhonna couldn't help laughing as her friend rearranged her hair. "Christmas isn't for six months."

"Well, your lunch with Mrs. Conway is today," Megan asserted, with one of her bizarre, unanswerable twists of logic. "Unless you want to call her and put it off till December 26th."

As it turned out, Megan was right about the mauve thing. Nobody had bought it because the hips were too small for most women with a 34 bust. Rhonna looked at herself back and front, thinking that if she had had the money and interest to hire a dressmaker, no one could have created anything that looked more perfect on her. She had the saleswoman cut the tags off and put her denim disaster in the fashionable Lily Paul's shopping bag.

"You'll have to wear my bone pumps and purse," Megan insisted, switching the contents of her purse to Rhonna's denim bag. Luckily, her shoes were only half a size larger than Rhonna's, a fact that had saved Rhonna from fashion gaffes more than once.

"But it's leather," Rhonna protested, holding Megan's elegant purse, with its "M" monogram, as far away from her as she could.

"But me no buts," Megan said, tucking the purse under Rhonna's arm. "The ecostructure will forgive you this once. If mother nature wasn't forgiving, we'd all be dead by now. You look fantastic, sweetie. Now go on. Knock the old lady dead."

Knocking Mrs. Conway dead was the last thing Rhonna wanted to do, the minute the hostess pointed out Cal's mother sitting at a corner table and staring out the window at an amazingly purple azalea bush. Ellen Conway's slender, small body had not been draped by Lily Paul, Rhonna could see at a glance. The older woman was wearing a pink sundress with a black linen jacket that could have been ordered out of a J. C. Penney's catalogue. Her neat cap of silvery gold hair shone in the light from the window, and so did her smile when she greeted Rhonna.

"You look wonderfully lovely in that color, my dear," she said, gesturing at the seat across from her. "But then Cal told me you look lovely in anything."

Oh, Lord, Rhonna thought, trying to read the other woman's look, *I hope he didn't tell her I was lovely when being kissed until I was comatose.* Cal could be expected to say anything that struck him at the moment, especially to this gentle, forgiving mother of his. Like her father, she guessed at a glance, Ellen Conway seemed able to understand and forgive whatever was thrown at her.

"Thank you," Rhonna said, trying to keep Megan's shoes from sliding off her feet as she arranged them under her chair. "You look too young to be Cal's mother."

"I've earned every gray hair he's given me," Mrs. Conway laughed. "My hairdresser tells me I should have given him up for adoption at birth and saved on the cost of L'Oreal."

Rhonna felt herself relaxing and smiled back. "Was he as hard to handle as a boy as he is now?"

Mrs. Conway scanned the menu and pointed out a chicken cashew salad to the waiter. "Oh yes. Demanding justice all the time. Having to be right. Actually he *was* right, much of the time. Not about God though. It broke my heart when he quit going to church."

"I'm not happy about that myself." Rhonna ordered the same salad, with iced tea. "It's hard to imagine Cal as anything but formidable. I'd like to know if he was always that way."

"I remember once when he was four or five and his cousins had taken over the toy box," Mrs. Conway reminisced, looking with soft eyes into the purple azalea outside the window. "Cal stood dramatically on a dining room chair, waved his arms for attention and roared to the whole family, 'We should all share toys!'"

Rhonna laughed, wondering if Cal remembered being an orator for justice as a child. "And when he was older?"

"A bulldozer was left on the hillside opposite our property," Ellen Conway said, folding her hands on the table and looking at Rhonna directly. "It was going to knock down a stand of trees the next day. Cal was about thirteen at the time. He went out with his father's tools that night and dismantled the bulldozer's engine. Threw the parts into the creek. His father was incensed at the bill. As I recall, he cancelled Cal's allowance for life."

Rhonna sipped her ice tea, watching the play of light across the fragile, slightly lined skin of Ellen Conway's mobile face, looking for something of Cal there and finding it in the full, sensitive mouth. "His war with his father goes back that far?"

"Farther. His father wanted to control Cal from birth. Mold him into the man he wanted to be himself. And I wanted him to be God's man. An old story." Mrs. Conway waved her hand, dismissing the problem. She obviously had long since made her peace with the war between father and son.

"You wanted my help, you said." Rhonna started to eat her salad, then put down her fork, wanting to give full attention to what Mrs. Conway would say. "I'll do anything I can."

Mrs. Conway munched a cashew thoughtfully, with obvious relish. "I'll be frank with you, my dear. Cal's gotten involved with this dreadful countess woman. Do you know anything about her?"

It was true then, Rhonna thought with a sinking heart. Even Cal's mother knew about Cristina and Cal. "I've met Cristina a couple of times on Malta," she said cautiously, not wanting to say anything behind another woman's back to the prospective mother-in-law. "I can't really say much about her. She's out of my league. Rich, beautiful, sophisticated. I think she's very attached to Cal. He seems to be attached to her, too. I think they're planning to get married."

She tried to make her voice sound casual and distant, but a slight tremor at the end made Ellen Conway look hard at her. Rhonna stared at her plate and choked down a mouthful of marinated tofu, hoping she wouldn't require a Heimlich maneuver from the waiter before the food successfully cleared her throat.

"Hasn't Cal told you all this?" Rhonna wiped her lips with her napkin and drew a deep breath, hoping the mouthful was safely stowed in her stomach.

"He called me from Paris yesterday," Mrs. Conway said. "I asked him about the magazine stories linking him and this woman. He wouldn't say much, just that that he and this woman had a lot in common."

"The countess seems to agree." Rhonna carefully swallowed another bite of salad, then put her fork down, resting her hand on the table. "They've planned to buy my father's house on Dune Road, she tells me."

Ellen Conway impulsively reached out to touch Rhonna's arm. "It's gone that far," she murmured, half to herself. "I can't believe she'd be right for him. You, my dear, you would have been an answer to prayer. Cal says you grew up here in Southampton. Was it in that house?"

Rhonna nodded, feeling the tears spring to her eyes, not able to speak for a moment. "Yes. I was very happy there. I can't bear to think of..." She brushed her eyes with the napkin, hoping Mrs. Conway wouldn't see the tears and wouldn't know she was mourning more than the loss of the house. "I don't think there's anything I could do to stop this relationship," she said. "If that's what you're asking me to do. Cal and I didn't part friends."

"That's not what he told me." Mrs. Conway said softly, pushing her half-finished salad aside. "He considers you very much his friend, and himself yours. He wanted me to tell you that."

Rhonna wiped furiously at a tear that had spilled on the lap of the mauve silk suit, hoping she hadn't stained it permanently. "Did he ask you to tell me anything else?"

"No, but I got the impression he's concerned that you may lose your place to Ned Peavey."

"You're sure he's not just trying to get hold of it himself, for him and Cristina?" Rhonna sniffed and wondered if it would be hopelessly bad form to wipe her nose with her napkin. *Probably it would be,* she decided, and rustled in Megan's purse for a tissue.

Mrs. Conway handed her one quickly. "That's what I don't know. As always, Cal leaves me in the dark. If you learn anything more, do you think you could call me?" Mrs. Conway's voice was tentative again, as it had been on the phone. She was not a woman who wanted to pressure anyone. Rhonna could see that.

"Of course I will," she said. "I'm happy you asked me."

"There are many things I would like to ask you, my dear." Ellen Conway's eyes were kind as she put a fifty-dollar bill on the tray the waiter had left and rose to go.

"Another time, if you can manage it. I've learned enough, for now, and I don't want to keep you from your father. Someday, I hope, you can meet Cal's father. He would like you, I know. Perhaps you would be forgiving enough to like him. Cal could use your good example. He was always such a wild sort of boy. Never wanted to settle down." She sighed, laid her hand for a moment on Rhonna's shoulder, then moved away from the table.

Rhonna watched the older woman leave, and finished her salad down to the last bite. She suddenly felt renewed and hopeful, as if her life had something more in it than sorrow and loss. Ellen Conway had a style about her, Rhonna reflected, a warm, easy style that made others feel comfortable. As she mulled over what she would tell her father about this meeting, Rhonna felt almost as happy as she had felt on Malta with Cal.

If only he was not his hard father's son as well as the son of this down-to-earth, unpretentious woman. If she could trust Cal as she trusted his mother, Rhonna thought, she would be happy enough to fly all the way to the hospital. She looked down at the tear drop and saw that it had dried without leaving a spot on the silk skirt. A good omen, she smiled to herself, leaving a five dollar tip to supplement Mrs. Conway's already generous one. She wanted the waiter to feel as good as Ellen Conway had made her feel.

Rhonna stopped feeling good as soon as she saw Ned's car in her driveway. That's right, she thought, make yourself right at home, since you've got the place sewn up. She tried to arrange her face pleasantly so he wouldn't know she was well aware of his plan. He was not sitting on the porch, she noticed with surprise. That must mean he'd walked right in as if he owned the place.

"A bit premature," she muttered, walking in through the open front door, resisting the impulse to slam it. She could hear his voice in the kitchen. Since she could hear no one else's, she assumed he was on the phone. Rhonna pulled Megan's tape recorder out of the purse, snapped it on, and tiptoed toward the kitchen.

Ned's voice was loud and clear. He apparently had no idea he was not alone. "Yeah, top rate Plutonium-235," he said. "You want to start an Islamicist revolution over there? I'd guess you need some tactical atomic weapons and uranium to do it. I talked to your second in command last week, and the deal's set to go as soon as the U.S. president signs that paper. My sources say tomorrow night. We'll have your uranium for you before you can say Jihad. You got my New York number? Better call me back there."

Ned hung up hard, as he did everything, and Rhonna scurried back to the front door. She slammed it shut and called out, "Who's here? Tell me now, or I'm calling the cops."

"Just me, baby." Ned sauntered in, his hands in the pockets of his expensive linen pants. "Hope you don't mind if I used your phone for a long distance call. Cell phones are chancy out here. Let's have a little slosh of something and talk."

Ned poured himself a drink of her father's after dinner cognac and sat in a sagging living room chair, spreading out his legs in a gesture so proprietary she could have smacked him.

"Like the way you look in that suit. Slinky. You look as good to eat as a candy cane." He smacked his lips, but Rhonna couldn't be sure it was over the cognac or the prospect of eating her up.

"Look, I know what you're after with my house," Rhonna said, turning her back to him so she could leave the tape recorder working on the hutch, behind the geranium plant. "Don't think I'm so stupid I don't know you're trying to take it away from me."

She folded her silk jacket neatly and laid it over the back of a chair. Her arms felt suddenly chilly and moist, even though the air was warm. Ned seemed to carry winter and clouds with him. She folded her arms close together over her stomach and shivered a little. Looking down, she saw that the ivory surplice top was low enough to show more of her than was safe. She reached behind her and tried to pull the back down a little, feeling too exposed for comfort.

Ned got up lazily and came over to her, standing too close. He looked down at her, his eyes half-closed. "Gorgeous one, I'd like to take everything I can get from you. And I plan to."

Before Rhonna could move away, his arms were around her, his fingers sliding on the silk of her blouse. Faintly, in the distance, she heard a car crunching stones down the driveway, but couldn't be sure if it was only her imagination. Probably just someone trying to turn around. She groped behind her for the geranium plant on the table, while Ned slobbered on her neck. If any man ever deserved to have a geranium pot broken over his head, this one did. In the movies, the maneuver looked easy, but it wasn't easy in real life. She frantically ran her hands over the table, not finding anything to hit him with. Maybe he would back off if she got sick all over him, which she felt was going to happen any minute.

Ned was getting excited, his heavy, damp red face shoving into her neck. One hand pushed under the edge of her blouse, which had pulled free, and the other held her jammed against the hutch. Rhonna turned her face away from him and screamed, as she heard the door open.

Over Ned's beefy shoulder she suddenly saw Cal's tall form in the doorway. He was across the room in a moment. Clutching Ned's shoulder with one hand, Cal pulled him around, and landed a punch to the heavy man's left temple. Ned sat down hard on the polished pine floor and looked surprised.

"No bodyguards around this time, Peavey," Cal snarled, in a voice so harsh Rhonna hardly recognized it. "I ought to tear your face off for what you've done to Rhonna. For what you did to Nancy. Don't think I'm not counting up the years I'd get for atrocious assault and deciding whether if you're worth it." He cast a quick glance at Rhonna. "I'm assuming you weren't into this scene just now, Rhonna, because that's what I want to believe. Set me straight."

"You assume right." Rhonna realized Ned had pulled her blouse out of her skirt and that one shoulder was bare and bruised. She tucked in the blouse with shaking hands. "Let him leave, Cal. It's okay."

Ned staggered up, gave Cal an unreadable look, then turned to her and said, "We aren't finished with our business yet, Rhonna. I'll expect your call in New York." He went out the front door, lurching against the frame and careening outside.

Rhonna leaned against the door when she had closed it. Seeing Cal again made her feel like she should lie down before she fell flat on her face. He was filling the room with his electric energy, walking toward her, taking over her space with every step. His square jaw was set, and the perpetual frown drew his dark brows together.

"Why didn't you trust me?" His words hung deep in his throat. "Feeney tells me you as good as gave this place away to Peavey."

"I was trying to save it," Rhonna said, feeling the silk of the surplice top slide off her shoulder. She laid her palms flat against the door behind her, wanting the security of what she had always known. "I didn't want you and Cristina to have it. Ned offered me a way out, and I took it."

Cal took a single long step forward, so that his body was only an inch from hers. He leaned against the door with his arms on either side of her as if he was suddenly exhausted.

"Look, Ned was the one that bumped your story from *Newstar*, so you couldn't get your money. He bought up your mortgage. What else does he have to do to show you what he is?"

"And what have you done?" Rhonna couldn't move. She was trapped in the small square Cal had left her and had nowhere else to go. "You want my home for Cristina. How do you think I feel about that? Or did you ever give a thought to how I might feel about her living here with you?"

She felt the words come out of her mouth involuntarily, as if she was spitting out broken glass. He had lacerated her. The word was not too strong. She would lacerate him back.

"For one thing, I haven't put your tape recorder in my pocket, which I might have done, if I'd wanted to take what you have on Ned." Cal put one hand behind her neck, massaging it under her hair, his eyes blazing into hers, his face an inch away. "I want you to know that since I first looked at you, not an hour has passed that I haven't thought about how you feel, how you look, how your body felt next to mine. And you don't know that? God, how can you not know?"

As he lowered his lips to her mouth, not allowing her face to move away, he wrapped one long, firm leg around hers, holding her still. His body shook as he pressed it against her, and she felt the power of his longing slash into her as if they were skin to skin. Her legs weakened under her.

"I only know what I feel," she gasped, moving her lips against his. "What you feel is a mystery. Always has been. If I knew you, things might be different, but I don't."

He pulled away from her and turned his back, not wanting to be known, she assumed. "You'll know me when you trust me, Rhonna. What else can I say?"

"You can tell me if it's possible to find out a long distance number if somebody has used his card and your phone to dial it." Rhonna slipped under Cal's arm and grabbed her jacket, feeling naked until she had put it on. His presence made her feel as if she was wearing no clothes at all. She wanted something to distance him and felt words were the only tool she had.

"Ned called somebody from here?" Cal's dark eyes narrowed. "Do you know what the call was about?"

"Not really." Rhonna felt embarrassed as she tried to tell the truth but not all the truth. *Lord*, she thought, *it's hard to be devious. Help me to find my way back to being honest, the way you want me to be.* "I just want to know how to find out who was at the other end of his phone call."

Cal relaxed a little and gave a shrug. "Okay. When someone's on the line, I'll hand you the phone. Maybe you'll get it that I'm on your side."

He dialed a few numbers and asked some questions. Then he handed the phone over to Rhonna. She snatched up a pen and copied down the information, saying nothing out loud. Ned Peavey had been calling a number in the Middle East. She didn't want to write any more than the number, in case Cal changed his mind and decided to track down Ned's contacts himself. The call had been placed to a Taliban warlord who was trying to take over his country from the elected government. All Rhonna needed to know was the warlord's name in order to nail down her story. She kept the information in her head and didn't write it on the pad by the phone.

"Well? Are you satisfied that I'm not trying to steal your story?" Cal stood behind her, and she could feel his warm breath on her neck.

"What story? You got the one that would have saved this place." Rhonna walked away, not wanting to turn around and face him.

"And you think Ned Peavey was trying to save it for you?" Call gave a harsh, uncomprehending laugh. "Rhonna, when you figure out who your friends are, give me a call at Feeney's. He'll know where to find me."

Before she could reach out to him, tell him she knew Ned Peavey was no friend, Cal was gone, out the door, and a few seconds later, she heard wheels spin on the gravel.

Chapter Eight

"Megan?" Rhonna tried to keep her voice from trembling over the phone. Megan would know right away something was wrong. "What do you know about Cristina Montani?"

Her friend's warm voice came racing over the wires. Megan loved to tell everything she knew, and being in the society network, she knew a lot. Rhonna could imagine Megan kicking off her pointed pumps and putting her feet up on the open drawer of her desk.

"Only the gossip," Megan said. "And there's plenty of that. Cristina's one of the ten best-dressed, and she didn't get there the easy way, by being married to a prince. Last year at Cannes she wore a dress that had spangles a half inch across, cut so low, or high, depending on which direction you start from, that the neckline just about met the slit up the skirt. The top was red silk alternating with strips of black voile, and the skirt…"

"Megan, I don't care if she was wearing a plastic baggie. Just tell me who her friends are," Rhonna interrupted. "Not the society ones. Business friends. Do you know? Can you find out?"

"Business. Let me think." Megan was quiet for a moment, and Rhonna could hear her friend's sharp nails, with the tiny diamonds inlaid at the tips, tapping on the phone as Megan concentrated. "Okay. I've got a name. Ned Peavey. My mother told me he's a buddy of the Russian mafia, into smuggling or something. I wouldn't know. Hey, girl, are you coming to prayer meeting with me tonight? I'm worn out doing your praying for you."

"It's about time I did my own praying," Rhonna answered. "Yes, I'll come."

Rhonna hung up only long enough to ring Bill Kingsley. He was silent for a moment after she'd told him the name she'd gotten from Megan and asked him for anything he knew on Peavey's mafia connection.

"You don't want to know," Bill said finally, his voice strained and hoarse. "This guy smuggles more than cocaine. He's into undercover weapons sales. Atomic weapons, they say. No proof, of course, or he'd have been picked up by now. And proof is what you'd need to make this story fly. Rhonna, don't take it any farther. If Ned Peavey's tied to the Russian mafia, you'd best back off."

Rhonna thanked him and hung up without saying what she was thinking, that if her editor had been brave enough to publish her story in *Newstar*, she wouldn't have to be hunting down every last dirty detail about Ned Peavey's connections with the underworld. She paced up and down the uneven bare wood floor of the hall.

Cristina and Ned had in mind to dig up American uranium and sell it to anybody overseas who would pay top dollar. That was clear. And Cristina's mafia friends were going to turn the uranium into weapons and sell them in the Middle East. Maybe all over the world, where the terrorists could kill American civilians. Rhonna's heart seemed to swell in her throat as she thought of the innocent lives that would be lost if these weapons were used and of the land that would be left bare and smoking, not to speak of the government forests Ned was planning to steal in order to get the uranium he wanted. And his threats against Cal's life. *I'll stop Ned Peavey,* Rhonna promised herself, *without Cal's help. God's help is all I need.*

After seeing to it that her father was fed and sleeping in his hospital room, Rhonna slipped out and went to church. Megan met her at the door and the two went into the sanctuary together. The last of the sunlight was turning the simple, colorful squares of stained glass into a glowing pattern across the gray carpet. Only a small number of people were present, as usual. Bill Kingsley was sitting in a front pew, with his oldest child next to him, just the way she remembered sitting with her father and mother years ago. Pastor Ken was beginning the scripture reading when she and Megan sat down behind the Kingsleys.

"Be ye therefore merciful, as your Father also is merciful. Judge not, and ye shall not be judged: condemn not, and ye shall not be condemned: forgive, and ye shall be forgiven. Give, and it shall be given unto you; good measure, pressed down, and shaken together, and running over, shall men give into your bosom. For with the same measure that ye mete withal it shall be measured to you again. Luke 6:36-38."

Pastor Ken paused and looked around the room with his piercing blue eyes, stopping on each familiar face as if he knew what was going on behind the usual pleasant mask everyone wore.

How she wished Cal could hear that verse, Rhonna thought. If he could just forgive Ned and his father, maybe his heart would open to God. Pastor Ken seemed to be looking directly at her as he ended the reading with a prayer. When the circle of worshippers formed around him for healing, Rhonna took a deep breath and asked for help.

"I need protection," she said, standing in the center. "I'm fighting the devil in the form of a very bad man. Please, pray for me, that I don't fall into his trap."

"Let us pray for our sister, Rhonna," Pastor Ken said, putting one hand on Rhonna's shoulder. The others crowded close to her, putting their hands on her back or on each other. Bill Kingsley and Megan stood closest, and Rhonna could feel the warmth and love flowing from them straight into her heart.

"By the power of Christ's name, I ask that our sister Rhonna be given protection against anyone who means her harm," Pastor Ken said, his voice deep and clear. "Lord, we ask your blessing on this child of yours that she may be kept safe in the arms of your Son, our Savior, Jesus Christ." He paused, then looked at her intently. "And may she forgive others as she herself has been forgiven. Amen."

Suddenly tears filled Rhonna's eyes. She realized that Cal was not the only one who needed to practice forgiveness. If she had been less judgmental of him, he might have found it easier to forgive his family. *Pastor Ken's right*, Rhonna thought. *I need to get rid of the log in my own eye before I go for the splinter in my brother's. And I thought I knew the Lord's Prayer. Maybe I'd better start practicing it.* Megan gave her hand a squeeze as they went back to their pew.

Frowning a little, Bill Kingsley watched Rhonna until she closed her eyes, not wanting to see him. If she confided too much in Bill, she thought, she might get him into trouble. *Better not to tell anyone the extent of my dealings with Ned Peavey*, she figured as she slipped out of the church before the final hymn.

She reconsidered before leaving for New York the next day. At least one person should know where she meant to go. She couldn't burden her father or Megan with that dangerous information. So she dropped off a note for Bill Kingsley at his office on her way to the station. She turned off her cell phone, not wanting him to call and pressure her not to see Ned. *I have to do this. Lives depend on it. Maybe Cal's life.*

All the way into town she thought about the missing link that was left, the linch pin for her story. What was missing was the name of the senator whom Cristina and Ned were working on, the man Cristina had taunted Ned with, on the balcony of the Gozo hotel. Whoever it was that had the power to promise her land to Ned might also be the one who was pressuring the President to sell Ned that uranium mine under the Adirondack forest. *Cristina wouldn't tell me, that's for sure. So I'll have to get the information out of Ned.* Cal wasn't the only one who could lay his life on his line for an important truth. Rhonna pulled out her cell phone and called Ned's Manhattan apartment.

Cal Conway had not been able to sleep all the way back from France on his expensive private flight, and now his eyes were burning in their sockets as he gripped the wheel of his rental car, trying to stay on the narrow lane between Sean Feeney's office and Dune Road. What Feeney had told him about Rhonna's virtually giving the property up to Ned Peavey hadn't made him want her any less. She was as innocent as Nancy had been, and as determined to make her own way. Ned could do to her exactly what he had done to Nancy. Cal felt his heart race when a sudden rush of adrenalin. This time, he would be there soon enough to help, not off on an adventure as it had been when Nancy had taken her own life rather than ask for what she needed.

The memory hurt too much, and Cal turned his mind away from it to Rhonna. He could still see her swirling in her rainbow-colored dress, her face close to his as he bent her slender body over his arm, her long dark eyelashes lying on her smooth, flushed cheeks when she closed her eyes rather than look into his. His hands tightened as he curved them on the wheel and remembered how soft her skin felt under them. He found himself actually praying, to his surprise, a prayer that came as creakily as an old door being opened. *God, if you're there at all, take care of my Rhonna. Don't let Ned Peavey hurt her.* He left the prayer unfinished, since he knew it was useless to bargain with God, but the rest of it hung in his mind—*if you save Rhonna, I'll be able to believe in you again.*

No wonder he hadn't slept since Paris, Cal thought, setting his lips in a straight, angry line, with his every other thought sliding toward Rhonna Moran, as if his whole world had been forcibly tipped in her direction. Her smile, even that one slightly crooked front tooth among all the regular ones, made him catch his breath, and he had to force his mind away from the image of her supple body dancing in his arms. At that moment, he had felt she was all his.

He shook his head at the words. She would never belong to him, not now, not believing as she did that Cristina and he were about to be married. And that he wanted the house she had grown up in to give to another woman as a wedding gift. With any luck, Cal thought, forcing himself to slow down before the local police could take twenty minutes off his already limited time, he would soon be able to tell Rhonna the truth.

Even though Rhonna had not gone with him to Paris as he had wanted, his time there had not been wasted. He had learned that Ned Peavey was digging uranium clandestinely out of the U.S. forest reserve in the Adirondacks and who Ned had been selling it to, with the help of a crooked senator who was one of Cristina's less savory friends. Her maid had let Cal into her mistress's Paris boudoir to leave a gift for his *promessa sposa*, as he had called Cristina, winning the heart of the romantic Neapolitan serving girl. She had curtsied, given him a key, and left him plenty of time to hunt down Cristina's business diary, which he finally found in a sequined evening purse under her heavily loaded shoe rack. She collected shoes the way his father collected guns, Cal thought. And she might better collect guns too, if she planned to go on dealing with Ned Peavey. Thinking of Rhonna's involvement with the same dangerous man made Cal put his foot harder on the gas, regardless of the local speed limit.

The diary had told him more than Cristina would have, no matter how skillfully pressured. In the countess's precise, even handwriting, were all the facts he needed to know. The hotel into which Cristina and Ned had been planning to turn Rhonna's house was going to be a mafia playground where the two of them could peddle their illicit atomic arms all over the world. The stakes were even bigger than he had thought. Cal's mouth grew tight and grim as he made a forty-five degree turn into Rhonna's driveway. Her truck wasn't there, which meant she had probably gone already. He left the car door open as he ran up the sagging wooden steps to the Moran's front porch.

When no one answered his pounding on the door, he opened it, shaking his head at Rhonna's carelessness, and called her name. No answer. She was likely halfway to New York by now. All the same, he would check upstairs. Taking three steps at a time, he hurried up the worn, carpeted staircase. He saw that one door was open off the hall, went in, and stopped. This room had to be hers, he said to himself, his eyes roving over the flowered quilt with her outline still pressed in it, her shorts on floor, the open perfume bottle on her vanity. Feeling strangely intimate with this woman whose place he had intruded into, Cal held the bottle up and took a whiff before absently putting the cap on. His head swam for a moment and he could have sworn Rhonna was in the room with him, her presence seemed so real. He had a sudden urge to put his face against her abandoned clothes, but instead laid them on the bed, trying to think. If she wasn't here, maybe she was at the paper. Another call to Kingsley would tell him.

His fingers hit the pushbuttons of his cell phone hard as he read the numbers aloud off the notepad beside the bed. The phone at the *Newstar* started ringing. Cal smiled at the large teddy bear sprawled face down on the floor. While he waited for someone to answer, he cuddled the phone under his ear, leaving both hands free to pull Rhonna's shorts onto the bear. He smiled again as he imagined her wondering how her stuffed animal had managed to get itself dressed. The smile vanished as the thought bore down on him that she might never come back to this room.

A voice answered and Cal took the phone with both hands, leaving the bear to fall over on its back. "This is Cal Conway of AP," he said curtly. "Get me your editor-in-chief."

He lay down on the bed, fitting himself to the indentation Rhonna had made, and kicked off his loafers. Cutting into Bill Kingsley's rush of compliments, Cal came to the point.

"Rhonna's not at her house," he said, pushing a thumb and forefinger into his sleepless, burning eyes. "Any idea where she's gone? I've got reason to think she may be in trouble."

"I can't believe she left home so fast," Bill Kingsley said. "She dropped off a note saying she was going to drive into Manhattan this afternoon and see Ned Peavey. I guess she knew it was dangerous, because she wanted someone to be in on where she was going, just in case. Left me the latest details for her story. She's onto big stuff." Bill Kingsley sounded as proud as a new father.

Cal swore under his breath. He might have known that a small town newspaper editor had no idea that his novice reporter had a tiger by the tail. "Look, I can't talk now," he said, elbowing the stuffed animal out of his way as he sat up. "Rhonna's in over her head. Don't let her father know. I'm going into Manhattan to find her."

"You think maybe we should call the New York cops?" Kingsley's voice sounded shaky now. "They can't do anything without a warrant," Cal said, getting up. "And we haven't got anything on Peavey at this point."

"I still think the cops would..."

Cal hung up in the middle of Bill Kingsley's anxiety attack, pulled a small black book out his inside jacket pocket, and looked down the list of addresses he had for Ned Peavey. His free hand curled into a tight fist as he thought of Rhonna at the mercy of the man who was responsible for Nancy's death, even though Ned hadn't personally pulled the trigger. Rhonna was too innocent to know what Ned Peavey was, Cal thought. She was too straightforward to imagine the tangle of murder and theft Ned had made of his life. Cal was not going to allow the man to drag Rhonna down any further. Imagining Ned's beefy, short-fingered hands on Rhonna's slender shoulders, his face mashing into hers, made Cal want to ram his fist through the wall. This time, this time, Ned wouldn't be allowed to have his way. Never again would Ned have his way if Cal could help it.

Nancy had fought Peavey off the only way she could. As she had seen her situation, it was either give in to Ned or check out. She couldn't face life without the land she loved so much and had taken the only option she had. Cal had loved the land too, but had dealt with its loss by throwing family and home away. His father had sold out the family and that swelling, snowy, precious Vermont land for the big bucks that had given him the prestige he had always hungered for. He wasn't all that different from Ned Peavey, and in his own way, was just as responsible in Cal's view, for what had happened to Nancy. That was another reason Cal couldn't forgive the old man and hadn't spoken a word to him in seven years.

On the table beside Rhonna's bed, he noticed her worn Bible. Behind it was a framed copy of the Lord's Prayer. She had underlined one word—forgive, and the word struck his heart. *God, let me be like her and forgive my father. At least, be willing to forgive.* Still, he could not put aside his anger. After all, Nancy was the only one with the right to forgive, and she was dead. He took the Lord's Prayer and laid it face down on the table, so he wouldn't have to look at it.

Cal snapped the address book shut and left the room, trying not to notice the lingering scent that almost drew him back. One day he would carry Rhonna into that room as his wife, he swore to himself as he bounded down the stairs. He would lay her down on that flowered quilt. Then he would show her, in the only way he knew, how much she mattered to him.

As he came to the foot of the stairs, the phone rang and he paused, waiting until the answering machine picked up the call. It might be Ned, he thought, in which case, he'd pick up the receiver and tell the man what was in store for him if he laid a hand on Rhonna Moran. Instead of Ned's voice, he heard his mother's, and he held his breath, listening intently.

"My dear," Ellen's soft voice hummed, "I need to ask your help again. Can you come to our house in Scarsdale for dinner this Friday night? I want you to meet Cal's father. And he wants to talk to you. We'll send a car down for you, if you wish. Call me back, please, as soon as you can. You have the number."

His mother's voice stopped abruptly, and Cal let his breath out. What was his mother calling Rhonna about? The two of them obviously had formed an alliance of sorts behind his back. He was not pleased at the thought of the people he loved most in the world having plans for him. All his life his mother had tried to get him to give up his travels, his "dangerous life," as she called it, and become a family man. She had begged him to go back to church with her. It had been a mistake to mention Rhonna to her during that call he impulsively made the week before. If Rhonna hadn't so totally occupied his mind, he might have been able to keep his mouth shut about her. But when his mother asked if there were any woman in his life, he poured out his feeling for Rhonna, unable to stop himself.

For all he knew, Cal thought angrily, his mother had plans to get Rhonna's help in bringing him and his father together. Not in this lifetime, Cal said to himself, slamming the front door behind him so hard the old house shuddered. Even Rhonna could never make him love the man whose lifetime dream was to cut his son down to manageable size. The two of them were on opposite sides of a war, and neither would ever surrender. His father's terms had been for Cal to give up travelling and find a job near his family or else. Cal was the only child now, and owed it to... The old man's voice would have droned on into eternity if Cal hadn't hung up on him, tired into flight by his father's manipulation. Cal's terms were freedom, absolute and unconditional, and his father would never meet them. Until Cal had connected with Rhonna Moran, those terms had dominated his life. No one was going to hook him into losing his freedom. Now he was revising his idea of what it meant to be free. Until recently, by not forgiving, he could maintain his distance from anyone who would compromise his freedom. *Once I start forgiving, there's no limit to the hold other people will have over me. They'll be close, they'll be wanting something from me, and I'll be stuck doing what they think I should do. No, better not to forgive in the first place* He would keep his autonomy, Cal said to himself, and his distance, forgiving no one who had done him wrong.

Strange, how easy it had been to forgive Rhonna, though, for misleading him about her reason for being in Malta. It occurred to him for the first time that if there is love, forgiveness came right along with it. But he pushed the thought to the back of his mind, afraid it would lead him into trouble.

At least no one knew, not even Ellen, that Cal had been offered the plum television news show of the decade, his own weekly foreign news hour, analyzing foreign affairs and operating out of

Manhattan. He had turned the job down since it would mean giving up his travelling. The network producer wanted him badly enough not to take no for an answer. The job would be held open for him indefinitely. Cal shrugged and put the thought aside. If the network wanted to wait, let it wait. Meanwhile, he had some living to do.

As he got back in his car, he wondered if Rhonna would ever be willing to travel with him overseas, living out of a suitcase as he did. Even as the idea came to him, he shook his head. *She would want to stay here, and who could blame her.* He looked around him as he drove down the long, serpentine driveway at the willows waving their pale green branches in the gentle breeze and the tall purple irises rising behind the low, irregular rock wall. No. Cal stiffened and kept his eyes straight ahead as he pulled onto the road. No. Rhonna would have to come with him. He would not settle, not even for paradise.

Rhonna's truck began to sputter alarmingly when she had driven as far as the Huntington station. She wondered if it felt the way she did, that this trip to Ned Peavey's was not to its taste. Rather than risk driving farther, she dropped it at a mechanic's and picked up the Long Island Railroad, the "Toonerville Trolley," her father called the noisy, bumpy railway, refusing to set foot on it.

As she sat staring out the window while the familiar landscape sped by, Rhonna wondered if Cal was so mad at her he would never come back. See my lawyer, he had said, if you want to get in touch. That sounded pretty final. Like something a man said at the end of a relationship, not at the beginning. He was clearly not the sort who would hang around trying to persuade her he was a nice guy. Either she trusted him or she didn't.

"But how could I trust you," she whispered, loud enough that the man next to her turned to stare. "How could I trust you when you and Cristina are getting married? Come on, Cal. I may be naive, but I'm not stupid."

She smoothed the soft mauve silk over her lap trying to calm herself. Maybe the trouble was, she thought, that she couldn't believe Cal could want anyone as ordinary and unexciting as she was. A countess, yes. Someone with a yacht. An adventuress, a glamor girl. *No way he could want me, Rhonna Moran, with my dowdy house, uncertain livelihood, and notions about living simply on the land.* Malta and Paris had moved her to tears, but what about the Paris of the heart, she asked herself, the place where you could find beauty anytime, in your own backyard? What she had always wanted was to build a life so rich inside that travelling and adventure would be beside the point. That was why she could never marry a man who based his happiness on this world, not on Christ's kingdom of mercy and love. *The two go together. Without love, you can't be merciful. You can't forgive. And that's where Cal is. I can't let myself get stuck there with him.*

If he wanted Cristina, Rhonna kept coming back to the bleak truth, he wanted something less than she herself wanted to give him. To her, an adventure was finding a starfish in a tide pool or an egg-filled nest under the eaves. A far cry from Parisian nightlife or gambling at Monaco, the world Cal and Cristina shared, to which she herself would always be a stranger.

Rhonna sighed and clutched her purse under her arm as she got off at the 42nd Street Station. *Times Square is no place to daydream, she told herself,* as she walked past the store windows full of jewelry and electronics. *Most of them were likely stolen. I'm already in Ned's world.* Not sure how to find his place by bus or subway, she hired a cab to take her uptown to Ned's penthouse overlooking the art museum.

He was comfortably sprawled on his couch with the inevitable drink in hand when he opened his front door electronically to let her in.

"Come in fast, gorgeous one," he said lazily, clicking the remote device in his hand. "You don't want to be in the way of that door when the beam closes it."

Rhonna heard a whirring sound next to her and moved fast as the door closed. Right behind it, a shiny metal panel slid shut. No one would get in here uninvited, unless he had a blowtorch, she thought uneasily, putting a hand to her throat.

"You look like a statue, standing there that way," Ned called across the room, his eyes glittering hungrily. "Come on in and I'll show you around my permanent collection. Maybe you'll be part of it sometime."

He poured her a martini, which she pretended to sip, then put down on the counter. Ned led her around the living room, stopping at alcoves and niches to show her the beauty his cash had bought him. As she looked at a gold-leafed Siamese goddess, Rhonna thought how much land had been ruined so that Ned Peavey could possess these treasures. The Siamese goddess looked sad and out of place. Her beauty seemed diminished by being trapped in this expensive chrome and leather dwelling.

Rhonna reached out a hand to touch the goddess, but Ned pulled her away. "Remember those caves I said my father discovered in the Adirondacks?" Ned pointed at a cluster of framed maps on the wall. "I promised you'd see them if you came to visit. Look, this one leads to the mine where...never mind." Ned drained his drink and pulled her down on a leather couch wide as a bed. "You had some more questions for me?"

He thrust his face close to hers and she moved back against the arm of the couch. "You said your father found radioactive material in that cave. I'd like to know more about it." Rhonna hoped her voice wasn't shaking the way her hands were.

Ned scowled and his eyes narrowed. "That's not for public information. If it turns up in your article, you'll be in major trouble. Here, let me take off your jacket. Your shoulders look so pretty when they're bare."

Rhonna slid out of his grasp and picked up the remote door control. "I've never seen one before," she said. "Looks just like the ten-key I learned at school. Show me how it works."

"Why not? Guess you haven't been around men like me much, wasting your time with news-grubbers like Cal Conway," Ned said. "With me, you can learn how to live, sweetie, not just survive. Like the idea?"

He pushed a four-number sequence which Rhonna mentally repeated to herself until she had it memorized. The door opened, and with another series of taps, Ned closed it again.

"See? That's power, gorgeous one." He grinned at her and laid the remote on the marble table behind them. "And I've got more where that came from."

He set a hot, exploring hand on her bare shoulder, and Rhonna pushed it away, crossing her legs tightly. She ran frantically through the agenda she had brought with her, hoping to think of something she could use to turn his attention away from her body.

"I thought the power lies with the government. Senators, for instance," she said, starting to get up. Her idea was to get him another drink, but this time, Ned set down his empty glass and held her hard by the wrist.

"You got a particular senator in mind?" Ned's voice growled deep in his throat.

"Not if you haven't." Rhonna smiled sweetly, deciding she had better back off from any more information-gathering. The way Ned's eyebrow was sharply crooked over one eye made her rethink the idea of getting information from him as a priority. The real priority was getting out of Ned's apartment intact. *Please God, let me not be in over my head. I surrender all this mess to you. Your will be done.* She wished she had made this commitment clear both to God and to herself before coming to Ned Peavey's apartment.

His face looked cold and hard, and he squeezed Rhonna's fragile wrist so firmly that she gasped. "Cristina's told you about who's getting our deal through to the President? Or was it Cal? Tell me."

"Look, I really don't know. Those two don't tell me anything." Rhonna's breath was coming fast and shallow. "I was just fishing."

"You were just lying." Ned pulled her closer and bent her arm behind her. "I know a few ways to make you talk, all of them a lot more fun for me than for you."

He pushed her other arm to the side, against the back of the couch where her fingers could touch the table behind it, and leaned over, pressing his heavy body against hers.

Rhonna let out a sharp scream before his mouth closed over hers. No one would hear her, she realized, but the sound cut through her throat involuntarily.

Suddenly she heard a pounding on the door and Cal's voice, muffled by the thickness of the panels. "Rhonna! Open up, Ned, or the police will open up for you." "The building cops'll put you down fast, Conway," Ned yelled back, taunting Cal. "But not before you get to hear everything I'm doing to this little girlfriend of yours."

Rhonna's fingers groped for the remote, her nails skittering on the slick marble surface of the table. Her mind raced furiously as she tried to remember exactly where he had put the device. It had been right behind his head, and by leaning back just a little more, she might be able touch it. There. One finger brushed the corner of the remote, but her hand was pushed away when Ned shoved her down into the couch cushion.

"Rhonna!" Cal's shout was despairing, and the wooden door shook, striking with a dull gonging sound against the metal.

Ned kept his face pushed against her bare shoulder as he grappled with her clothes. He leaned hard against her, pinning her other arm under her so that her wrenched shoulder ached. Still, his heavy hand did not loosen on hers, and her fingers hovered tantalizingly, maddeningly, over the remote. Only one thing to do, she thought, remembering how a possum had saved itself from her collie, many years ago, in the woods behind their house.

She let her whole body go limp, as if she'd fainted. Ned involuntarily responded by letting go of her hand, devoting himself to pulling up her skirt. Rhonna was not able to see what she was doing, for Ned's body pinned hers flat on the leather sofa. But her fingers remembered where the numbers were. She mentally thanked her father for having insisted she take that business course where she had learned to work a ten-key in her sleep. For a moment she froze, as the last number eluded her. When she heard Cal's frantic voice call her name again, she remembered, and struck in the missing digit.

The door and metal panel slid open, and over Ned's shoulder, she saw Cal bound across the room. Ned was too involved with her skirt to realize Cal was in the room, until the tall man had shoved him off Rhonna, then pulled him to his feet. Cal kept his knee braced on Ned's thigh, while he whipped a sudden punch to the heavy man's nose. As Ned sagged to the floor, Cal's fist swung again and caught him hard under the jaw. Ned's teeth crunched together, and his eyes crossed as he went down, landing on the glass and chrome coffee table. The glass shattered as he collapsed onto it. His body hung grotesquely in the chrome square, arms and legs hanging outside the frame.

Cal's eyes blazed into Rhonna's as he picked her up off the couch. He ran his hands over her, straightening her clothes. "Woman, you had me so scared, I actually prayed. Seems like God heard me."

"What about him?" Rhonna nodded at Ned's unmoving form and his smashed, bleeding nose. "Is he dead?"

"I doubt it. The world should be so lucky." Cal pushed at Ned's foot contemptuously with his own. "We'd better get ourselves out of here before his goons show up. They're never far away."

"I need to take something first," Rhonna said, puling reluctantly away from his encircling arm. "This map." She unhooked the framed, rough-edged piece of yellowed paper from the wall. "It shows where the uranium cave is."

"We'll need that to prove uranium is what he's after. Good job, Rhonna." Cal broke open the back of the frame and slid the map out. "Here. Put this in your purse. We haven't time to look at it now."

He grabbed the remote with one hand and her elbow with the other. "We need to go. I hear voices down the hall."

Once they were in the hall outside the penthouse, Cal handed the remote to Rhonna."Hurry. Punch in those numbers again."

Her fingers trembling, Rhonna forced her mind to resurrect the series of digits she had learned from Ned. Just as the door slid closed again, three men ran around the hall corner toward them. Cal slipped the remote from her hand into the pocket of his crisply pressed ivory linen slacks.

"We heard yelling in there," he explained calmly to the three heavyset men, who looked like clones of Ned Peavey. "Can't figure out how to open this door."

"Yeah, we heard something on the monitor," one man said, frowning at him. "Don't I know you from someplace, dude?"

"Sorry," Cal said smoothly, moving off down the hall and pulling Rhonna with him. "Haven't had the pleasure."

Leaving Ned's security men pounding on the door and calling through it to their comatose boss, Rhonna and Cal ran to the elevator. Before they got in, Cal shoved the remote device deep into the sand of the cigarette urn beside the door.

"It'll be a while before they break him out of there," he smiled grimly at Rhonna. "Whenever it is, it'll be too soon to suit me." Rhonna stood carefully away from him in the elevator, looking down at the floor. She was remembering that the last time she had seen him, he had told her to talk to his lawyer. "You knew about the uranium all the time," she said. "Why didn't you tell me?"

"We're competitors," he said lightly ushering her out the door into the parking area. "Or so you seemed to feel back on Malta. Here, too. I don't remember you handing me over any crucial information, my love."

Rhonna blushed at his last words, even though they were said with a sarcastic edge. "I get the feeling there's a lot I don't know. You might have trusted me, Cal."

"I might have, if I hadn't observed you were typing twice as much into my computer as my printer was printing," he said, steering her into a red convertible and slamming the door after her. "You think I didn't know you had an agenda?"

Rhonna stared down at her lap, smoothing the wrinkles Ned had forced into the soft, mauve silk. They came out immediately, as if he had never touched her. She could see Megan's point about not buying cheap clothes.

"I had no choice," she murmured, not wanting to look at him. "You know that. And because you knew it, you tried to grab my dad's land." She looked straight ahead as he drove up the steep parking ramp to the street. "For you and Cristina. Ned told me."

"I just bet he did." Cal swung the car north, up the East Side Highway, not answering for a while. He kept his eyes on the road, and the little muscle moved in his tight jaw.

"Why are we heading north?" she asked as they crossed the bridge into the Bronx, and after a while switched onto the curving, forest-lined Saw Mill River Parkway. Shaded, roadside streams rushed past them, and she noticed that the gentle meadows rimming the road rose and fell like the terrain at home in the Shinnecock Hills.

"You have a date with my parents," Cal's voice grated. "Or don't you remember your cozy relationship with my mother? It's been a busy day."

"You're angry that she and I are friends. Is that it?" Rhonna tried to keep her voice calm, wondering how he knew about her meeting with Ellen, wondering if he was angry with her for snooping behind his back. Knowing how he felt about his parents, she would not be surprised if he felt betrayed by her once again.

"No." Cal glanced at her and briefly ran the backs of his fingers down her cheek. "I'm angry that we don't trust each other, that I'm going to have to speak to my father, and that there won't be any time between now and after dinner to get you alone."

"Oh." Rhonna couldn't think of anything else to say, and kept her head turned toward the window. She watched the little white bridges and flowerbeds fly by them until the car turned off at the Scarsdale exit. She finally blurted out what she was thinking, just as they were swinging into the circular drive in front of a three story Georgian house, with a rose garden in front, its tall, peach-colored roses swaying against the white stone background of the porch.

"I wish you'd tell me why you want to make out with me when you're about to marry Cristina. Is that too much to ask? Just be straight with me," she pleaded in a shaking voice. "If it's just sex, I want to know. It's not just that for me. I promised God that I would make a Christian marriage, and I keep my promises."

He turned off the engine and his arms swept her into their circle. "So do I. That's why I can't tell you everything now," he whispered, his breath tickling her ear, making her skin prickle. "When the story comes out, it'll be ours. The first byline I've ever shared."

He wouldn't let her answer, but touched his lips to her mouth, nuzzling it like an impatient, loving animal, the way her young foal had when it wanted to be fed. His hands ran down her back and he pulled her toward him. "I wish I had the words to tell you how much I want you," he said, his lips moving on hers. "I want to kiss every part of you."

"Children?" Ellen's gentle voice sounded from the sweeping veranda. "We've been waiting so long. Please. Come in."

"Damn," Cal muttered, slamming his hand against the steering wheel. "Family. When have I ever been glad to see them?"

Ellen was wearing a long, delicately flowered peach silk gown, which she gathered around her as she ran down the steps to the car.

"My dear girl! I wasn't sure you got my message." Ellen hugged Rhonna, gathering her into a fragrant embrace.

"Mother." Cal got out and gave Ellen a quick kiss on the cheek. "You have this wonderful talent for showing up in the middle of things."

"My dramatic instinct," Ellen smiled, taking Rhonna's hands. "Did Cal tell you I studied to be an actress? Then I married Cal's father and gave it up."

"Don't believe a word she says." Cal stayed close behind them as Ellen led Rhonna up the steps. "No one could have stayed married to my father without being a consummate actress."

"Cal, please." Ellen turned to him with a beseeching look. "It's been seven years since you've talked to him. Be kind."

"Seven and a half," Cal retorted, holding open the heavy, carved oak door. "But who's counting. Rhonna, stay beside me. If I get savage, give me a nudge. The old man's sixty-eight. It's something I need to remember, along with your forgiveness prayer."

Rhonna nodded, wondering how Cal knew about the prayer she kept at her bedside. She stepped between Cal and his mother as they walked into the house. As they went in, he tossed his car keys on the foyer table. For a moment, just inside, she paused. Though the outside of the house was old-fashioned, inside, it had been modernized by some decorator who apparently had specialized in skyscrapers. The entrance was walled with pale Swedish oak and skylights overhead let sunlight into the slate-floored foyer, large as her living room at home. A wide, concrete circular staircase curved upward twenty feet on their right, and the living room opened to the left, revealing an expanse of charcoal gray carpet and metallic furniture. Rhonna glanced around her, thinking that Ellen must have chosen this house, with the trade-off being that her husband could gut the interior and turn it into an environment suited to his executive tastes. The whole place looked to Rhonna like a very expensive office.

"Welcome." A tall, slender man stood in the center of the room, supporting himself on a metal cane. "I wish I could assume you're responding to my invitation."

Rhonna wondered whether Cal's father meant that they were not particularly welcome or that he would have preferred they had come because they wanted to. In either case, she felt the chill of his hard, controlling stare and of Cal's stiffening next to her. Would Cal be like this someday? Too rich, too strong, too hard? She threw an anxious glance at him, a little reassured by the way he stepped sideways and took his mother's hand. No one said a word for a moment, but Ellen and Cal exchanged a look that said to Rhonna, 'nothing has changed.'

Drawing a deep breath, Rhonna walked up to Mr. Conway, her hand out. She looked straight into his piercing, heavy-lidded dark eyes.

"Hello. I'm Rhonna Moran," she said, shaking his hand. "I hope we can be friends." She meant all four of them, but would settle at this tense moment for just Mr. Conway and herself.

"You're Cal's intended?" Mr. Conway's grip was limp and uncommitted, but at least he didn't pull away.

"Not exactly." Rhonna let her hand fall to her side. "I mean, I'm not sure who that might be. Right now, I'm thinking we'd better start off without labels. I'm a friend of Cal's and would like to be a friend of yours. That's all."

The old man slumped a little. "I have very few friends," he began uncertainly. Then he straightened again. "But I would like you to be one of them. Come, Rhonna." He took her arm. "We're about to have high tea on the terrace. I would like you to sit beside me."

Rhonna allowed herself to be led out through tall French doors to the wide flagstone terrace behind the living room. Her eyes wandered over the lush greenery, the waterfall that had been artfully constructed beside a little bridge. The walkway would take a visitor into a maze of ferns and flowering pink azaleas. Clearly, Ellen ruled the décor of the garden, as thoroughly as Mr. Conway determined the interior of the house.

"My dear, you come innocently into a nest of serpents, I'm afraid." Mr. Conway said, pulling out a curlicued white iron chair for her at a large, round glass table. "I trust you come equipped with anti-venom."

Rhonna saw Cal shrug and roll his eyes. He was distancing himself, unwilling to be part of the scene. She could feel him pulling away, even from her. Still, the old man was a part of him, part of the dance they were trying to do together. She would do what she could to make the dance work.

"We've just come from a bad scene," she said, leaning toward Mr. Conway, fixing her eyes on his. "Forgive us if we aren't at our best. Cal knocked out a pretty important person. Ned Peavey. I'm afraid Ned will send a hit man after him. I understand that's happened before."

Mr. Conway looked hard at his son, then began shifting the head of his cane from hand to hand. "I've told you, Cal, that it's no good going after people like Ned. One of these days he'll put you underground, and the world will be poorer for it. Yes, it will." The old man looked down and rubbed the corner of one eye vigorously with his linen napkin.

Rhonna half-turned and saw Cal was staring at his father in surprise.

"You don't want anything to happen to Cal. Is that what you're saying?" Impulsively, she laid her hand over Mr. Conway's.

"I've lost one child to that man," the old man said, a quaver in his voice. "I don't want to lose another."

"You see, Cal!" Ellen handed a tray of cookies at her son, then put it down again when he made no move to take it from her. "It's because he loves you that he wants you to end this vendetta with Peavey."

"Yes." Mr. Conway jabbed a finger in Cal's direction. "Why don't you take that job in New York? Don't you think I've tried to get you settled? Safe?"

Cal pushed back his chair and stood up. "Nancy wasn't safe. You let her die when Peavey called the mortgage on her land."

"That's not fair!" Ellen's face was white, and she seized Cal's arm. "Your father grieves every day of his life that he didn't know what Nancy would do when she lost her land. He didn't want to interfere in her financial affairs. She'd told him not to."

Mr. Conway held both hands tightly over the head of his cane, then brought his forehead down on them. "I'll never forgive myself for what happened to her. Never." His voice caught in his throat. "I don't expect that anyone but God will forgive me."

Rhonna reached over and put her arm over his thin, shaking shoulders. She tried to imagine how her own father would have wept if he had known himself responsible for her death. Tears sprang to her eyes. "What happened was terrible," she murmured, putting her face against Mr. Conway's. "But it's not your fault. You didn't know what she'd do."

She looked up at Cal's pale, remote face. "Please, tell him it wasn't his fault. End this thing between you." Her eyes stared deeply into his and her voice shook.

Cal looked warily at his father. "You and I should talk," he said at last, and waved the women into the other room. "Rhonna, stay the night. You and I need to talk, too. I've had a lot on my mind. It's time to unload." He raised his hand in her direction as she walked with Ellen toward the garden. "Don't forget what I said in the car. There's too much still hanging in the air."

Rhonna glanced behind her at him as she went with his mother over the narrow bridge toward the garden, glad to see his eyes linger on her, even as his hand dropped to his father's shoulder.

"Is it true Cal could have a job here in the States? One that would keep him safe?" Rhonna stopped on the bridge, holding the rough wood railing tightly with both hands. She stared down at the bubbling stream, then let her eyes follow it until it wound into a small pond, where orange fish darted up to kiss the surface.

"His father got him the job," Ellen said, twisting the long sash of her gown in nervous fingers. "The network was happy about it. They didn't know Cal was interested."

"Is he? I'm afraid he'll be really mad that his father stepped in." Rhonna shook her head. She wanted to believe that somehow Cal could be anchored and safe, but something didn't feel right to her. If Cal was boxed in he'd flee as he always had. Like his sister, he wanted no one interfering in his life. And if he should decide to marry, how long would it last, once his wanderlust took hold of him?

"I'm afraid so too. You know him well already." Ellen sighed and tucked her hand under Rhonna's elbow. "Let me show you to your room. I've been working on it ever since we met. This is one room that I didn't let my husband take over."

They went up the winding metal staircase together, and Ellen opened a door at the end of the hall. "Look. I remembered that you like mauve."

Rhonna caught her breath and ran to the middle of the room. It was exactly what she would have created herself, if she had had the money. A large four-poster bed faced the open French doors onto a balcony. Rhonna could see across the expanse of white tiled balcony floor to the garden and pond below. In the distance, forest slopes rose into low-lying clouds.

Looking down, she saw the rose and dark green circular carpet that picked up the pattern and colors of the quilt and of the two cozy stuffed chairs that stood in the alcove of a bay window. Between them was a round white table on which Ellen had placed a Tiffany lamp and a few books. Rhonna noticed that one of them was a Bible.

Ellen opened the closet door and showed Rhonna a dresser and the doorway into a dressing room and bath. Even the towels were mauve and white. Rhonna half- expected to see her own initials on them, but Ellen had restrained herself in that, at least.

"If you need any clothes or toiletries," Ellen said, "please ask me. I see you've come with none of your things. But I'm so glad you came at all. Here's the key to the room." She slipped the key into Rhonna's pocket.

Rhonna took Ellen's thin hands in hers. "I'm glad, too," she replied. "And never mind about breakfast. I'll have to leave early in the morning. My father's getting out of the hospital tomorrow."

"And you'll be picking him up?"Ellen turned back the covers and smoothed them down.

"Wouldn't trust it to anyone else," Rhonna smiled, seeing Ellen to the door. "Please. Tell Cal I'm taking a nap before supper."

Or was it dinner, she asked herself frantically, wondering what people like Cal's folks called the evening meal. Whatever it was, Ellen seemed only to be glad she could expect Rhonna to be there.

Of course, she thought, taking off her suit and shoes and lying down under the soft, fluffy quilt, *Cal might bound up the stairs at any moment, in a fit of fury with his father, and insist on leaving.* As her eyes drifted closed, Rhonna wondered if she would be roughly awakened and ordered to leave with Cal. *Or perhaps,* she thought, *I'll be waked by his lips on mine, his arms around me* Thinking that he might come in, she forced her eyes to stay open for a while. As she stirred on the soft sheets that matched the quilt, one hand reached under the pillow and found a sachet Ellen had placed there. Raising it to her nose, Rhonna savored the scent of roses. How had Ellen known it was her favorite? The afternoon light outside the balcony dimmed as the sun set beyond the mountains, and Rhonna fell asleep, wishing Cal would visit her room and afraid he would.

Chapter Nine

Ellen, not Cal, knocked at her door when it was time to eat. Cal was still talking with his father in the study, but Ellen was about to insist they join the women for dinner. At least, she said to Rhonna with a nervous laugh, they hadn't come to blows and Cal hadn't stormed out for another seven years of silence.

Mr. Conway sat at one end of the long chrome and glass table. He insisted that Rhonna sit on one side of him and Cal on the other.

"You've softened my son's heart a bit," he said to her, unfolding his large, white linen napkin. He laid it on his lap and smoothed the sharp creases. "But we still don't agree about that job in Manhattan."

"I'm not a man for office work," Cal declared. "Never even considered it."

But at least his voice was calm and his face was as serene as Rhonna had ever seen it. Even the little twitch in his hard jaw was gone. He looked at Rhonna between the array of ivory candles in silver holders of varying heights. Without saying anything, he kept his eyes on her face, and she felt herself turn pink. She could feel his gaze touch her soul and pour through her, melting her like the wax of the candles that pooled in their silver holders. His look told her that he wanted to touch her, probe her depths, and intended to. Rhonna looked down at the ratatouille a maid put in front of her. She tried to imagine how it would feel to have Cal slip under that soft quilt with her, blending his breath and life with hers, and her hand shook as she took up her fork. *He's not the marrying kind,* she told herself, *and God knows I couldn't bear for him to love me and leave me. Lord, protect me from that. Better I should lose him now. But not my will, only yours. . ."*

It seemed to her a long time until the dessert plates were removed and the last of the after-dinner cognac was sipped to the bottom of the tiny crystal snifters.

"So, my dear," said Mr. Conway, "Cal's explained to me about this wretched countess." His eyes lit on her kindly, and he seemed not to notice how red her cheeks had turned. Cal was touching the bridge of her foot with his toes. He had apparently kicked off his loafers and was massaging her calves without his expression revealing in the slightest that any such thing was going on under the elaborately set table.

"That's more than he's explained to me," Rhonna retorted, tucking her feet safely under the chair.

"The woman had information he needed for an important story. As long as she believed they were headed for the altar, he could depend on finding out what she knew." Mr. Conway glanced at Cal. "Why didn't you tell Rhonna, son?" His eyebrows came together in the same hard line she had seen Cal's form. "You stood to lose a lot by not telling her."

"And a lot by telling her, too." Cal shrugged, pushing his empty cognac glass away. "It was a judgment call. I must admit, I was holding my breath." He smiled across the table at Rhonna, and his face was suddenly young, his smile broad. "In our business, my love, you learn how to keep your mouth shut. You aren't so bad at it yourself."

"I guess we need a little trust. . ." Rhonna said, then trailed off as her eyes met his burning ones.

"All we ever needed around here," Ellen finished for her and leaned over to pat her hand. "And trust is one way of saying faith. I don't like to preach, dear," she said to Cal, "but without faith in God, I don't think we can put our trust in people."

"You're right, mother, as always. Rhonna and I have to trust each other if we're going to have a future together. But just now, we have a story to write," Cal said resolutely, standing up. "I'll get my computer. Dad, we'll need to use your study."

As the story unfolded between them, Rhonna almost forgot that she was alone with Cal at night for the first time since they had left Malta. The words poured out, from him, from her, and sometimes from both at once, as they flung ideas back and forth, catching half-thoughts from each other in mid-flight. They played back her interview recording with Ned and his call to the Middle Eastern jihadist. The senator's name would be out there, finally, for the public to see.

"Not likely now, that the President will sign that bill," Cal said, flipping off the recorder. "He'd lose the whole Northeast in the next election, and his advisors will tell him so." He smiled grimly as he punched in the direct quotes that should put Ned and the senator behind bars, if justice were done.

"We'll print Ned's map?" Rhonna asked, typing out the last sentence of the article.

"Yeah, that's essential evidence. But forget about including the Russian mafia names," Cal said, pulling the sheets out of his father's laser printer. "I want to live long enough to get married."

"I thought you had no plans along that line." Rhonna raised an eyebrow.

"You know better than that," Cal said, not looking at her as he laid the papers in the fax machine and punched in his editor's number. "Do I have to fall on my knees?" He whirled around and seized her by the shoulders, searching her face as if to find his answer.

"I can't imagine you doing that. You don't have to. Being married to you is what I want." Rhonna reached up timidly and curved her hands around his face, feeling the rough stubble under her palms and the throbbing at his temples.

He didn't say anything, just pulled her against him, his arms shaking a little, and buried his face in her hair. For the first time, she felt not so much his passion, but his love. Though he could not speak, she knew what he wanted. This time, he was not demanding, not wearing her down, but touching her more deeply than he ever had, reaching for a place in her heart. She felt as she once had when a young mountain lion whose foot had been caught in a wolf trap had laid his head on her shoulder while she freed him.

"It's all right," she murmured, half-thinking that she spoke to the lion again. "It's all right. You'll be free. I promise."

He withdrew a little but kept his eyes on hers. "I'm afraid freedom is a word I no longer understand."

"You will," Rhonna whispered. "You will."

Arms wrapped around each other at the waist, the two went upstairs to the room Ellen had prepared. Rhonna ceremoniously folded the quilt down. As Cal turned off the overhead light, she switched on the tiffany lamp, which embraced them both in a living rainbow.

"I've been thinking," Cal said, sitting beside her on the bed. "Admittedly, it's hard to do when you're so close to me."

"What?" she asked, wondering how thinking might be possible, given her own pounding blood and spinning head. "Thinking what?"

"I'll have to take that idiotic TV job my father got for me." Cal kissed her forehead, her eyes, the tip of her nose. "It's the only way."

"You'd hate it." Rhonna tried to struggle upright, but managed only to land on her side, her body tight against Cal's. "I don't want you stuck in a cage."

For a moment he was mixed up in her mind with the young mountain lion that she had freed rather than see in captivity. It would almost be better, she thought, to lose Cal now than to see him grow angry and distant over the years, as the frustration grew and his horizons shrank. The fear she had felt in the back of her mind since she had first met this man suddenly rose up like a monster and darkened her vision of him.

"I have no choice." His voice was soft and inexorable against her ear. "There'll be children. We'll need to live a settled life."

"Not if you don't want to." Rhonna felt a hard knot in her stomach. "Look, I won't be responsible for making you give up the way you need to live. You do a lot of good, and you need to keep on doing it. And in time, you'd resent me. I know you would."

Cal lay back on the flowered pillows and put one hand over his eyes. "I don't know about all that," he murmured. "All I know is that I love you. I'll do whatever I have to do in order to make a life with you."

Rhonna rose quickly and grabbed the purse she had left on the night table. "I won't let you," she whispered, feeling a slicing pain in her chest as she said it, knowing there was no other way than a clean split. For a moment she stood still and felt something freeze and crack inside her. *This is what it feels like for your heart to break.*

"It's not right. Rhonna almost choked on the words. "Better to stop now, while the love's there than to see it die a slow death. I said before that we don't live in the same world, and it's still true. We don't."

She ran out of the room before Cal could stop her, closed the door hard and pulled the key out of her pocket. Before Cal's body slammed against the door to force it open, she had turned the key in the lock. She left it there so that Ellen could let him out later and ran down the wide curved staircase, sobbing. More than her own happiness was at stake, she said to herself as she scribbled a note, telling Cal that his car would be at the White Plains railway station. He was a man who could make a difference in the world, and she would not selfishly allow herself to get in the way of it.

She stopped at the front door and took in the realization that she actually loved Cal better than she loved herself. This moment proved it to her. She almost went back upstairs, absurdly wanting to call through the door to Cal that now he knew how much she loved him. Instead, she ran outside and started the car, then looked up and saw Cal gesturing and calling to her from the balcony.

"Goodby," she called back, knowing her voice was too thin and weak to reach him, as his was to reach hers. "Goodby, dear one. I will love you all my life."

As she headed down the serpentine drive, she foresaw how dreary that life would be without Cal. A projection unreeled before her into the future, and the images seemed faded and worn even before they happened in real time. Still, she knew what it would be like to see him caged and angry, the way he had been as he entered his parents' house. He wasn't meant for her kind of country life, she thought, swinging the wheel wildly to avoid a porcupine dazzled by her headlights in the middle of the narrow road. *I have to let Cal off the hook. Someday he'll be glad of his escape.* Rhonna had been a Christian long enough to know that sacrifice was better than selfishness.

To feel Cal's impatience, his longing to be somewhere else, when she was doing everything she could to make him happy would be an agony she wasn't up to. He lived for change, and she had fought change and loss since she could remember. In the end, she would have wound up fighting him and seeing the love in his eyes harden into cold remoteness. Better to be the one who left than the one who *was* left. *But for the rest of my life,* Rhonna said to herself, *I'll remember the warmth of his arms and the sudden flash of his wit. It will have to be enough.* She cried all the way home on the train, not caring who saw her.

Rhonna woke up on the couch in her Southampton living room the next day. She had been too tired to make it up the stairs after the long train ride from Westchester County in the middle of the night. What woke her up was the thud of the *New York Times* being delivered on her doorstep. She carried it into the kitchen with her, staring at the right hand column. It was a story with her name and Cal's as the by-line. Reading it as she drank a glass of orange juice, Rhonna smiled a little, a smile that was sad and ragged at the edges.

"Dad's going to jump out of his skin," she said aloud. "He's going to be one happy convalescent."

Her smile died away as she remembered what she had done the night before. Given up Cal. His proposal. His offer to sacrifice his career for her. *Dummy,* she said to herself, her heart heavy and sore. She shook out a handful of vitamins and gulped them down. *You had what you wanted, right at your fingertips, and you gave it up.*

The dead certainty rose in her again that she had given Cal up because she couldn't bear the possibility that he would ever again look at her without love. At those moments when he had been angry with her, she felt an unbearable sorrow and terror. To go through life in such pain as that, or under the threat of it, would hurt too much. A small voice surfaced in her, asking insistently, *but doesn't the loss of him hurt even more?* She shook her head and forced the voice into the depths again.

Not wanting to think any longer, she opened the paper and laid it flat on the table, but found it impossible to read the familiar words. All that spun around in her brain was the fact that she had given Cal a way out. Now he could say to his parents, to himself, that she had turned down his best offer. And he would be off to Paris or to the Amazon, where he would forget her before the plane touched down. She wanted him to override her objections, wished he would. But that was unlikely. If he hadn't called by now, he wasn't going to. If he had loved her, really loved her, he would have come after her, or at least called. As she had suspected last night, his talk of love had been the result of a moment's romantic excitement. In the light of day, Cal must have realized that his sacrifice was absurd, unlivable. And he would go somewhere, anywhere else, to start over.

The phone rang harshly and she jumped up, knocking over the kitchen chair. Was it Cal, she wondered, her heart pounding as she ran down the hall.

"Great work, Rhonna," came Bill Kingsley's voice over the phone. "A by-line with Cal Conway. You're in the bigtime now. Hope you'll still work for us."

"Of course I will. You know that." Rhonna looked at her face in the mirror over the telephone table and winced at how pale she looked. "One story with Conway does not a foreign correspondent make. Besides, I doubt there'll be any more where that came from."

"Well, then," Kingsley laughed his gasping laugh, "you'd better get cracking on your Peavey interview. Word just came over the wire that Ned Peavey fell off his Manhattan balcony at 7 AM this morning. Landed thirty stories down, smack on his head."

"Drunk, probably." Rhonna put down her glass of juice, feeling too queasy to drink anything.

"Goes without saying. But my guess would be some of the mafia guys hit him. Your story spilled half the spaghetti, and they wanted to be sure he doesn't spill the rest."

"I'll fax you a piece of my *Fortune* article as an obit," Rhonna said. "You'll have it in a few minutes."

She hung up with shaking hands and sat down hard on the telephone bench. Suddenly her eyes opened wide in fear. If Ned Peavey was lying in the morgue, who owned her property? She ran upstairs to get dressed fast, hoping Sean Feeney would be in his office. She needed a lawyer, and Cal's would be better than anyone. If what she remembered from Cristina's conversation with Ned on that Maltese boat was correct, Cristina was now the owner of her house.

The first thing that struck her when she went into her room was that someone else had been there. Cal. She could almost feel his presence, and took in a sharp breath as she saw the slight indentation on the soft mattress, too long a mark to have been left by her. Then she saw the half-dressed teddy bear and smiled a little.

"It's the story of our lives, Teddo," she said in a low voice. "He was here and I wasn't. I'm here and he isn't. That's just how it would be if Cal and I tried to make a life together. So it's just you and me, Ted."

Holding the bear tightly under one arm, she lay on her bed, carefully positioning herself into the dent left by Cal, and put the phone on her stomach. Her hands were shaking almost too much to dial Feeney's number, and she had to start over twice.

Sean Feeney was in court, his secretary said, and couldn't be reached even by cell phone. So Rhonna decided to go to the tax office. There had to be a way she could stop the transfer of the property herself. She put on her white jeans and dark blue tank top, pausing to look in the mirror as she zipped up. This was how she had looked when she had met Cal less than two weeks before, except that then her face had been rosy and now it was ashen. And her hair had been pinned up in back, under at least partial control, while now it swung wildly around her shoulders. *The way he likes it,* she thought, shrugging. *Not that it matters now.*

Wondering how she was going to be able to avoid having Cal sneak into her mind at every weak moment, Rhonna hurried down the upstairs hall. *Each day is going to crawl by*, she said to herself, taking the stairs two at a time as if to move the day faster, until finally, someday in the dim future, she would not wake up with Cal's name on her lips, the memory of him against her, skin to skin. *People say that time will heal everything. I've read it in books.* But it seemed to her now that time would stretch to eternity before she could forget the touch and look of Cal Conway. All the way to city hall, she thought resolutely about money, so as to avoid Cal's image searing itself on her mind.

The man who headed up the tax collection department for Southampton looked vaguely familiar to her, and she smiled uncertainly as she introduced herself to him. His face was sallow, and he kept pushing his horn-rimmed glasses up on his nose.

"I know you from way back," he said in a cold voice. "It was you who got me bumped off the water board three years ago. Remember me now?"

"Yes. I remember that you had just come to town." Rhonna swallowed hard. "I guess you got in with the wrong people." *I won't apologize for getting this crook bumped,* Rhonna said to herself, *however much power he has over me* now.

"So what can I do for you?" The man smiled with tight lips, not showing any teeth.

"I want the due date on our property tax extended somehow," she said in a rush, leaning forward, her hands on his polished desk. "The person that holds the mortgage was going to pay them, and he's dead now."

"So we heard." The man kept smiling as he talked, as if he was enjoying the words. "That's why we pushed the proceedings forward. The bank turned the property over to the new owner this morning. An Italian lady, I believe."

Rhonna gasped. Cristina's lawyer must have been in touch with them the instant Ned Peavey's head hit the pavement. *How had she known so fast?* "You can't do that," she cried. "I still had a few days left."

"A technicality," he replied. "Your check didn't clear. Apparently whoever gave it to you withdrew the funds. In such cases, we proceed immediately with the transfer." "Look, I've lived here all my life."

Rhonna slammed one fist down on the desk.

"There must be something you can do. My family's had that land for a hundred years."

"Not anymore, they don't," the grinning, sallow man said as he got up to open the door. "Not anymore."

Rhonna ran out of the office, her heart pounding. So this was what she got for whistle-blowing. Kingsley had warned her at the time that she could get hurt, but the thrill of making a difference had driven her to get the story out. She had no doubt that the tax man had engineered the premature transfer of her property to the bank, maybe that he had been bribed to do it. He was obviously glad he could get back at her for bringing him down. *Is this the way the world will always be run,* she wondered, swallowing the lump that threatened to burst in her throat. Cal had as much as told her that for every exposé he wrote, somebody would like to see him dead. Still, he kept telling the truth and so would she. *Be wise as serpents,* Christ said, *and innocent as doves.* Since He was the one who said that, there had to be a way.

At the bank, she got the same story. All they could promise was that the house would be held in escrow for a month until Ned's will was read. Then Cristina would take possession. Rhonna tried to keep from crying as she drove to the hospital. She had looked forward so much to bringing her father home. Now she was going to have to tell him there wasn't really any place to come home to. Not for long, anyway. All because she hadn't trusted Cal as he had asked her to.

She stopped at the cardiac nurses' station. "Is Mr. Moran ready yet?"

The nurse looked surprised and tapped her pen against her fingernails as she spoke. "And who are you?"

"His daughter." Rhonna tried not to show her exasperation. *What did they think? She was trying to kidnap Ed* Moran? Everybody in town knew how little they'd get for a ransom. "I was told he would be ready to go home today."

"Well yes, he was." The nurse frowned and flipped through her register. "A fellow came and got him. Said he was a relative. Mr. Moran went right along, so I had no reason to think there was anything..."

Rhonna turned and ran out the door, her heart racing somewhere up around her throat. *What if Ned Peavey had sent somebody after dad to get back at me? What if the man who came for him hadn't known Peavey was already dead? What if the Russian mafia had heard from Ned or Cristina that they could shut me up by grabbing my father?* She kept her teeth clenched tightly together so she wouldn't scream out loud. Cutting through the back end of town, Rhonna took a short cut home, bumping over an empty field in order to pick up Dune Road past the traffic light. She had to get to a phone. Maybe Cal wouldn't want to talk to her, but she had no one else to call. The cell phone was too erratic to work this far out of the city, so there was no use trying it.

Swerving into her driveway at thirty miles an hour, Rhonna almost hit a shiny black BMW with a gold monogram. Whoever it was had pulled right up to the porch steps. She could hardly squeeze around the car to go up them herself.

She called inside as she opened the front door. "Who's in there? Tell me who you are."

Under the archway into the dining room, a tall, shadowed form emerged into the hall. Rhonna swallowed hard and couldn't move. The man was wearing sun-faded jeans and a blue work shirt turned up at the cuffs. The expression on his face was cool and remote, as if he was waiting for her to call the shots.

"Cal. I was going to phone you for help," she said in a small, tight voice. "Somebody's kidnapped my father." Her words ended in a wail, and she ran forward, throwing herself into his open arms.

"Easy, sweetheart," he murmured, holding her close and smoothing her hair. "Not every scene in this world is plotted in hell. I brought him home myself. Figured you'd be sleeping off our farewell drama."

"How did you...um, get out of the room?" Rhonna kept her face against Cal's shirt, taking in its piney scent, glad not to have to look at him.

"No use trying last night," he said. "Mother would have waked up and had a fit that you were gone. I got a good night's sleep in your bed and climbed across to her balcony at dawn. She was as astonished as Juliet, I can tell you."

"And my Dad?" Rhonna smiled, imagining Cal scaling the vines over the front of the Georgian house just as he had climbed down the sheer Maltese cliff.

"I took him upstairs. He's asleep. Told me to wake him when you came in."

"Did you?"

"No. I wanted you to myself." He tangled his fingers in her hair as he pulled her toward him. "It's about time."

Rhonna let herself be enfolded in his arms, the will to stay away draining out of her. Burning hot streams of energy prickled up and down her body, which suddenly became so weak Cal had to hold her tightly, to keep her from falling.

"You look so different," Rhonna murmured, her lips feeling uncoordinated, her words slipshod and slurred. "You look like people from around here."

"I figured it might be the clothes I wore that put you off," Cal said, running his hands up and down her back, straining her close to him. "It had to be something."

He took her by the shoulders, held her at arms' length, and stared down at her, the little muscle working in his jaw. "What is it that makes you run away, Rhonna? You think you're not good enough? That I want someone better than you? Hey, woman, you're the best there is. What do I have to do to make you believe that?"

"I want to believe." She let her arms fall to her sides, trying to think how to answer him. A swarm of thoughts buzzed in her head, none of them good enough reasons to offer him. Suddenly one idea brightened at the depths of her mind like gold in the sand.

"I know why it is," she answered uncertainly. "It's because I can't bear it when anything good changes. I know it's stupid, but that's how I feel. Like I'm scared to death my dad's about to die. Scared of losing this house. Scared of losing...you." Her voice fell to a whisper. "It breaks my heart when beautiful things are lost. That's hard for you to understand, I know. You like novelty. You expect everything to change, and you don't care. I live in eternity, you live in the world. How could two people so different manage together? How?"

He put his hand gently under her chin and tipped her face up toward his. "You think I don't know my own mind by now? Give me credit for that, at least. I never had a reason to like the way things were until I met you. Now I'd like to hold tight in my fist every moment I spend with you and keep it safe. Make it last."

He bent down and gently grazed her lips with his, keeping his eyes on hers. "That's what marriage is to me. I guess I'm growing up. Being a Christian is like being a complete person, a grown-up, which is probably why I've always avoided it. You've been teaching me why I shouldn't."

She pushed his hand away and looked down at his grass-stained tennis shoes, not wanting to look at his face. "You feel that way now, but in five years? When you're stuck in the country with a boring job and kids hollering at you to take them down to the pond? Me hollering at you to diaper the baby while I make dinner?" Cal grinned and held her close again, rocking her a little from side to side, as if she was a child. "Doesn't sound so bad to me. I'll take the TV job. What I do with my days doesn't matter to me so much as what I do with my nights." His arms tightened around her. "What we do. I've imagined it so much, sweetheart. There's not a part of you I haven't explored in my mind."

"Cal, it makes me scared, how much you know me already," Rhonna whispered, her lips moving under his. "I can't hold myself back anymore. I can't. I want you like I want my next breath. More." She pulled him closer, and buried her face in his chest.

A woman's cool voice spoke from the doorway. "*Scusi*. I am so sorry to interrupt this delicious scene. But I am the bearer of bad news. Not bad for me, *capisce*? Bad for you."

Cal let go of Rhonna and automatically thrust her behind him, as if to protect her. "Cristina. Tactless as always. Come to claim your goods, I'd guess."

"And you are right as always, darling," she purred, pulling at the hem of her sequined jersey, so that the already low neckline dropped another inch. "This house is not at all to my taste. I fancy a villa here, once the house has been torn down. Spanish or Tuscan style, with marble steps down to the sea. You will tell me your preference, Cal? No?" She walked toward him, hips swaying, her long, slightly slanted eyes on his.

"My preference, Cristina, is that you should get the hell out of here," Cal growled at her.

Cristina's smile and large teeth vanished. "*Basta.* Enough. I'll live in this place by myself," she snapped. "Or find a man who appreciates the good life I can give him. You and this kitten of yours," she spat out the words, "can leave now or a month from now. It makes no difference. You are, as they say, history." She turned on her high, tottering heels, and tossed her dark tangle of curls over her shoulder.

"Just a minute, Cristina." Cal strode over to her and swung her around toward him by one arm. "You'll tell your lawyer I'm buying this place from you."

Rhonna stood looking from one of them to the other, her hand over her throat. It was her home they were talking about, she said to herself unbelievingly. The place where she had slid down the banisters, played dolls on the porch with her friends, ridden her first horse. And she was helpless to decide what would become of it. Her hands shook, and she turned to grip the railing beside the stairs. As the shock of Cristina's words penetrated her, Rhonna realized how little of her life she controlled, how much she had to depend on Cal for what she needed, and on God for what her life would ultimately turn out to be.

The realization struck her not painfully, but with joy. *It's all right,* she told herself, almost dancing at the thought. *I can trust him, just the way I trust my father and God.* Cal loved her. He really loved her, with the kind of love he could learn only from God. She could feel that love in the air around her, running hot through her body like lava streams. Just as she would do anything for him, so he would do for her. She had guessed, hoped, longed, for this to be true. Now she knew it like she knew the sun would come up out of the sea every morning. Circumstances might change, but not this love that was raining on her, through her.

"Thanks, Cal," she said softly. "Thanks with all my heart."

Cristina stared at her, eyes scornful and blazing. "You think I would give this place up for anything?" she cried out. "For you two?"

"I think you'll give it up when you hear I wrote down every Russian mafia name in that Paris diary of yours." Cal's tone was even and menacing. "It wouldn't take me long to convince any one of those men that you had told me exactly what plans you had made with them for shipping weapons-grade uranium out of Rhonna's private beach cove. Maybe you'd like your head splattered on a Manhattan sidewalk like Ned's? Or maybe," Cal spoke softly and slowly, "maybe you're the one who pushed him off that balcony? You think the police don't know you were there?"

Cristina's face clouded and her voice turned shrill. "You know about those names? You dared invade my privacy?"

Cal's voice rose, with laughter under it. "You, my dear Cristina, have no privacy. Or honor. See my lawyer in town. Sean Feeney. He's already in touch with yours. The price is fair. Take it and run, is my advice."

"And you will destroy that list of names?" Cristina was trembling, and her words came out in a tight squeak. "No one must know."

"For once, I'm throwing away a story that my guts tell me should decorate the front page of the *Times*," Cal said, gripping Rhonna's hand in his. "You'd better leave before I have an attack of professional regret."

Cristina ran as fast as her stiletto heels would let her, and a few minutes later, they heard her car screeching its way up the pebbled drive. Rhonna laid her hands on Cal's forearms, feeling the wiry dark hair curl over her fingers.

"You bought the place for me," she whispered. "You saved it."

"Our place now," he said, drawing her closer, kissing her forehead, her cheeks, her mouth, with his burning lips. "And our kids', and our grandkids'. Down the line. As long as you want this to be home, Rhonna, That's what it'll be." He looked around at the faded wallpaper and shrugged, smiling. "And it'll stay this way, if you want. Unlike my parents, I'm not into interior decorating."

"Actually," she giggled, snuggling up close to him, "I'd thought of asking Ellen to re-do the house. It could use her talents."

"Just so you know justice is being done," Cal said, one arm tightly around her. "Cristina will be indicted for Ned's murder. She'll find out as soon as she talks to her lawyer. And if the justice system doesn't take her out, the mob will."

Rhonna shuddered. "She really killed Ned?"

"That's what his goons told the police. They said she was the only person besides Ned to have a remote entry device that would let her into his apartment."

"But why would she kill him?"

"Once she had possession of your house and the beach cove," she didn't need Ned." Cal explained. "And she was afraid he'd sic the mob on her, which he probably had in mind to do."

"As long as the mob doesn't come after you," Rhonna said. "Can we be sure they won't?"

"They don't know yet that I have the names in Cristina's diary," Cal said, "and that Feeney has the list in his safe. If they decide to go after her, they won't ask her any questions before they do whatever it is they're going to do. My lawyer talks to theirs, love, and nothing but sweet words pass between them. Feeney knows how to protect my backside. He's been doing it long enough."

"I wouldn't want to be Cristina," Rhonna whispered. "I'm sorry for her."

"I guess we have to forgive her," Cal said, both hands on either side of her face. "If I could forgive my father, it shouldn't be hard to forgive Cristina. Ned, I don't know about. That might take a while. My mother always said that with God all things are possible, and I'm beginning to believe it."

As the current heated and flowed between them, Rhonna felt the urge to find a place, a nest, wild and open to the sky. Her heart pounded against her ribs and she couldn't speak. She pulled him by the hand, out the back door and down the long path behind the house, a path winding to the sea below. He didn't speak, just let her lead him wherever she wanted to, his hand firmly around hers. "This is where I first saw you," Cal whispered, keeping his eyes on hers. "I loved you then, when your body was just forming its woman's shape, and I love you now. Oh my love," he whispered. "How I've wanted you. Will always want you."

"And will have me," Rhonna said, running her arms over his broad back.

Her eyes followed two mating raptor birds flying across the sky, out to sea, as they darted and plunged, not seeming to notice the sky or waves, only each other. "The time will come when we'll travel again. Work together."

"I'd like that. I think God made us for each other." Cal whispered into her ear. "We work well together."

"Together," she answered, turning his face so that his lips were on hers again. "That word tastes so good."

" 'Always' tastes even better." He kept his eyes on hers with a fierce intensity, as if he was afraid she would disappear if he took his gaze off her for a moment.

"Always." They repeated the word at the same time, then held each other so tightly that Rhonna wondered if she would ever breathe again. He began to kiss her mouth, her neck, and a deep breath tore miraculously through her like a long-awaited storm releasing rain, as her body followed her soul into a place she had never known before, where God ruled, and she was glad to let Him.

Also from SpiritBooks

Yeshua's Dog:
A Gospel Love Story

by Barbara Rogers

Illustrated by Tamaris Johnson

When a dog decides to follow Jesus Christ through his ministry in ancient Israel, we see what real devotion looks like. Human followers doubt and betray the Master, but his dog is there for him until the end, sharing his sorrows and his joys.

Yeshua's Dog is a reverent and vivid re-telling of the Gospel story, one which will inspire readers of all ages.

$8.50 U.S.
$9.50 Canada
ISBN 978-0-9834956-0-4

www.ingramcontent.com/pod-product-compliance
Lightning Source LLC
Chambersburg PA
CBHW072003290426
44109CB00018B/2111